PRAISE FOR
THE COACHING BOOK

"Whatever your role, everyone needs a sounding board to help them order their thoughts, challenge their thinking and inspire their new goals. *The Coaching Book* is a valuable handbook, expertly showing the important role coaching plays in empowering people to be the very best that they can be."

Mike Saunter
International Chief Financial Officer,
Clear Channel

"When leaders coach well, it's clear to see how it drives engagement and motivates individuals to be the best that they can be. This book adopts a step-by-step approach to help you practically apply coaching as a skill in and out of the workplace."

Janie Links
HR Director, Trainline

"This book is packed with easy-to-apply coaching tools and techniques to help you unlock your team's potential and maximize their performance so you can stand out from the competition."

Duncan Macdonald
Chief Information Officer, UPC

"Nicole's books are an inspiring and practical read and *The Coaching Book* is no exception. Her straightforward style and pragmatic approach to coaching provides you with lots of handy examples and exercises to use to develop a coaching style of management. I'm delighted to recommend this book."

Kate Buller
Director, Executive Coaching Company

"Coaching is an absolutely vital tool every leader must have at their disposal if they are committed to fulfilling the potential of their individuals and ultimately their team. With *The Coaching Book*, Nicole Soames takes you on a journey to develop your coaching skills with confidence, clearly demonstrating that when coaching is properly applied, not only will your team fulfil their potential – but everyone will realize that they can go so far beyond what was ever thought possible!"

PJ Bain
Chief Executive Officer, PrimeRevenue Inc

"The larger your teams grow, the more important it is to empower and equip them to make their own decisions. This book is packed with easy-to-apply coaching tools and techniques to help you unlock your team's potential and maximize their performance so you can stand out from the competition."

Chris Wallis
Senior Director Sales, Expedia

Published by
LID Publishing Limited
The Record Hall, Studio 204,
16-16a Baldwins Gardens,
London EC1N 7RJ, UK

info@lidpublishing.com
www.lidpublishing.com

A member of:

BPR
Business Publishers Roundtable

www.businesspublishersroundtable.com

© Nicole Soames, 2019
© LID Publishing Limited, 2019

Printed in Latvia by Jelgavas Tipogrāfija

ISBN: 978-1-912555-53-6

Cover and page design: Matthew Renaudin

THE
COACHING
BOOK

PRACTICAL STEPS
TO BECOMING A CONFIDENT COACH

NICOLE SOAMES

MADRID | MEXICO CITY | LONDON
NEW YORK | BUENOS AIRES
BOGOTA | SHANGHAI | NEW DELHI

FOR OTHER TITLES IN THE SERIES...

CONCISE ADVICE LAB

SMALL BOOKS: BIG IDEAS

CLEVER CONTENT, DYNAMIC IDEAS, PRACTICAL
SOLUTIONS AND ENGAGING VISUALS –
A CATALYST TO INSPIRE NEW WAYS OF THINKING
AND PROBLEM-SOLVING IN A COMPLEX WORLD

conciseadvicelab.com

CONTENTS

INTRODUCTION

"We cannot teach people anything; we can only help them discover it within themselves."

Galileo

In today's world, it's more important than ever to constantly upgrade skills and adapt to new ways of working. The pace of technology and innovation is accelerating – standing still is not an option; in fact, it's the fastest way of moving backwards. It's no longer about what you studied before you began your career; the focus is now on adopting a growth mindset and creating a lifelong learning experience that allows you to stay ahead of the game. Coaching lies at the heart of this learning experience.

Given today's unprecedented rate of change, it's not surprising that coaching has gone from the latest business buzzword to a fundamental business tool that drives employee engagement and performance. More and more organizations are committed to creating a coaching culture that encourages continual learning and development as opposed to the traditional annual performance appraisal process.

A conversation once a year just isn't enough – it's the conversations you have during the other 364 days that really count. As a manager or leader, it means developing a new range of coaching skills and techniques that equip you to have confident coaching conversations that motivate your people to achieve their full potential and maximize their performance.

1. WHAT IS COACHING?

First things first, it's worth clarifying exactly what the term 'coaching' means. In the corporate world, you will often have one-to-one meetings where you 'brief' or 'tell' your team what they need to do. These line management sessions differ from coaching conversations, where the focus *should* be on helping the other person, the coachee, work out what they can do differently. As a commercial skills trainer and coach who has built a business helping people set themselves up for success, I define coaching as **helping the coachee discover a new way forwards to fulfil their potential and maximize their performance.**

A powerful way to understand what coaching best practice looks like is to think of coaches from the sporting world. Their goal is to help athletes reach the top of their game and sustain their performance by working with them to achieve incremental gains – whether it's by helping them adapt their training plan, change their mental attitude or increase their confidence levels. Their role is to minimize their own personal agenda in order to uncover the specific needs of the athlete. Confident coaches recognize that coaching can act as a catalyst towards positive change, but ultimately it is the individual's responsibility to improve their own performance, whether it's on the sports field or in the business world.

People often confuse coaching with mentoring or managing. The diagram below illustrates where the role of the coach sits in a learning and development environment.

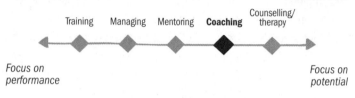

DIRECTIVE

NON-DIRECTIVE

Training Managing Mentoring **Coaching** Counselling/therapy

Focus on performance

Focus on potential

The role of coaching

If we start from the left-hand side, we can see that:

- Training is highly directive and performance-focused; it is about knowledge transfer and skill development.
- Managing involves the day-to-day briefing of tasks or projects with a focus on telling people what needs to be done so they can deliver results.
- Mentoring is about offering your expert advice and sharing your experience to help the other person improve their performance and reach their potential.
- Coaching is non-directive; it is about empowering the other person to find a way forwards that works for them so they can unlock their full potential.
- Counselling or therapy focuses on the present and past – unlike coaching, which is future-focused and solution-orientated. It also predominately deals with mental health issues and wellbeing.

As people in general – and millennials in particular – become increasingly resistant to being told what to do, it is clear that the old-fashioned management systems are no longer working. As a result, the non-directive nature of coaching clearly holds the key to creating a positive learning environment that encourages individuals to thrive and develop. Coaching provides a 'safe' environment where individuals can set new goals and ask for support without the fear of looking 'weak' in front of their peers. It also enables you, as a manager, to give your coachee meaningful feedback in a way that does not make them feel as though they are being singled out or criticized.

The term 'coaching' encompasses a wide range of approaches – the most common ones include:

- Confidence coaching
- Performance coaching
- Commercial skills coaching
- Relationship coaching
- Career coaching
- Executive coaching

It is your role as coach to identify what type of coaching your coachee needs at a given time. However, it's important to remember that for coaching to be effective over a sustained period of time, it needs to be blended with training, managing and mentoring. People are complex and need different support at different times of their lives. The skill of a confident coach is being able to use judgement to decide *when* to manage, mentor or coach the other person. By wearing different hats in this way, the coach is far more likely to be able to help the other person reach their full potential.

2. WHEN SHOULD YOU COACH?

I'm often asked when people should be coached and, generally, I recommend that it's whenever you feel that someone is stuck and not achieving their full potential. You need to bear in mind that the person may not even realize they are being held back, which is why I believe a manager is often the most effective person to coach people in their team. After all, you should know your people best and be able to notice when there is an opportunity to help them move forwards. The key to coaching is acting as soon as the opportunity arises – if you wait, it will be less effective.

Coaching can take place on a formal or informal basis. Take, for example, a colleague who confides in you that they often lack confidence in meetings and asks whether you can informally coach them to help them banish their imposter syndrome once and for all. Or perhaps you have been given feedback that someone on your team has upset a customer without realizing it. You decide the best course of action is to suggest some formal coaching sessions to help them improve their relationship skills so they can move forwards.

It is generally more straightforward to begin the coaching relationship in the first scenario, when someone has asked for coaching and is already aware of the potential benefits. It can be more challenging when someone has a blind-spot, as in the case of scenario two, as they may view coaching as a sign of weakness. In the latter case, the person could feel that coaching has been 'forced' upon them; you will therefore need to draw on your empathy to understand their mindset so you can help address their concerns and change their perspective.

I'm a big believer that you can coach anyone – as long as there is chemistry. You need to be able to connect and this requires mutual respect. After all, if you don't get on you are going to find it difficult to have confident coaching conversations. So, if you are asked to be someone's coach and there is no rapport, don't be afraid to pull the ripcord. You need to be able to challenge the other person's thinking, so it's critical that they respect and value your opinion. Remember, as the adage goes, "Popularity is temporary, respect is timeless." Confident coaches rely on their judgement to coach the right person with the right conversation at the right time, but more about exactly how to do this in the following sections.

3. EMOTIONAL INTELLIGENCE IS THE KEY

Research[1] shows that the secret to greater success in life is emotional intelligence. People with high levels of emotional intelligence – the ability to recognize, understand and manage their emotions and those of others – are more likely to build meaningful relationships with others. This is a skill that I believe is absolutely critical to becoming a confident coach. The great news is that your emotional intelligence, unlike your IQ, isn't fixed and can be developed over time. However, it takes hard work and commitment as these so-called 'soft' skills are often the hardest to learn.

The diagram on the next page breaks down emotional intelligence into three core coaching areas. Let's examine each of them in turn to identify exactly what skills you need to develop in order to have confident coaching conversations.

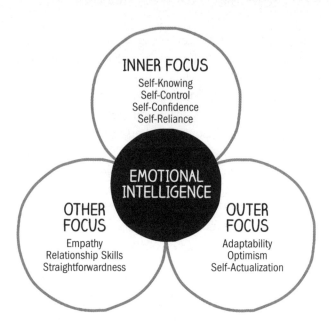

INNER FOCUS
Self-Knowing
Self-Control
Self-Confidence
Self-Reliance

EMOTIONAL
INTELLIGENCE

OTHER
FOCUS
Empathy
Relationship Skills
Straightforwardness

OUTER
FOCUS
Adaptability
Optimism
Self-Actualization

The Inner Focus circle: Develop self-knowledge to understand exactly what makes you tick so that you can recognize your personality type and the impact you have on other people. Then, drawing on your self-control, you can make sure you are truly present in the moment and can focus on the needs of the other person. Finally, it takes confidence and courage to challenge the other person's thinking and self-reliance to back yourself and believe that you are the right person having the right conversation at the right time.

Moving on to the **Other Focus** circle. Draw on your empathy to put yourself in the other person's shoes, listen beyond the words and understand their specific challenges. Then use your relationship skills to find common ground, build rapport and establish trust with them. It takes straightforwardness to have the difficult conversations and say what needs to be said. This means being prepared to have honest and open conversations.

Finally let's examine the **Outer Focus** circle. Adaptability is an essential attribute for a confident coach. You need to be open-minded and able to have a fluid conversation. It takes optimism to keep moving the conversation forwards – after all, you need to believe there is a solution. Lastly, you need to experience a sense of fulfilment from helping motivate other people to achieve their potential in order to be self-actualized.

Hopefully, this brief overview of the core emotional intelligence skills confirms just how inseparable emotional intelligence and coaching actually are. Coaches with high levels of emotional intelligence have the self-confidence and self-control to remain impartial, the empathy and social skills required to build strong relationships, together with the adaptability and optimism needed to encourage others to reach their goals. Coaches with low levels of emotional intelligence, on the other hand, are less likely to be able to adapt to different personality styles and are more likely to end up telling their coachees what to do instead of empowering them to work it out for themselves. Throughout this book, I will give you the tools and techniques to take each of your emotional intelligence skills to the next level so you can achieve real coaching success.

4. THE JOURNEY TO BECOMING A CONFIDENT COACH

As the Chinese proverb goes, *"A journey of a thousand miles starts with a single step."* Becoming a confident coach doesn't just happen overnight. Research shows that it takes 10,000 hours of deliberate practice to become world class in any field – and the same holds true of coaching; it takes dedication and hard work to take your coaching skills to the next level. The great news is that with this book, you have already taken that first important step on your journey to becoming a confident coach. This book will act as a guide to support you along the way by providing practical tools and exercises to help you unlock your emotional intelligence so you can coach with confidence.

In my experience, most coaching books on the market focus on the theory and treat coaching as a stand-alone skill. In my opinion, this fuels the common misconception that 'those who can't play, coach'. My mission is to set you up for coaching success by helping you adopt an integrated approach to coaching that allows you to draw on your empathy and experience to coach in an authentic and credible way at the appropriate time.

I have deliberately tried to de-jargonize coaching by breaking it down into bite-sized chunks that can be easily applied to daily life. I will work with you to help you develop a coaching mindset, build rapport and trust, adopt a disciplined approach, manage yourself during the coaching conversation and create momentum for change. This book has been designed to be used as a workbook – so don't be afraid to jot down notes and prompts as you read each section. By completing the different exercises and following the expert advice, you will be well on your way to becoming a confident coach who can move seamlessly from giving feedback and uncovering blind spots to action planning and identifying next steps to change behaviour.

PART ONE

DEVELOPING A COACHING MINDSET

The first step on your journey to becoming a confident coach is to develop a coaching mindset. This is a mindset that looks for the potential in others. This is easy to say but hard to do. As a manager, you have competing demands on your time and it can be tempting to prioritize pressing deadlines rather than focusing on the long game and developing your people. It takes a real shift in mindset to make it your priority to inspire and motivate your people to be the best that they can be.

A powerful way to transition from manager to confident coach is to remember the saying that, "Behind every fearless athlete, there's a fearless coach who refuses to let them be anything short of their true potential." This means focusing on the positives and believing that everyone can grow and develop with the right support and encouragement. In general, people will rise to your level of expectations. But if you pigeon-hole someone as stuck in their ways or only prepared to do the minimum, chances are they will continue down this road. Whereas if you believe that everyone can change their behaviour and improve their performance, you will look for opportunities to help them make this a reality.

1. THE IMPORTANCE OF PERSONALITY TYPE

How easily you can shift to a coaching mindset will depend to a certain degree on your personality type. It's important to remember that people are predictably different. All of us fall somewhere along the axes of *outgoing* to *reserved* and *task-orientated* to *people focused*. The DISC model below, first outlined by psychologist Dr William Marston in his book, *Emotions of Normal People*, illustrates this in greater detail by breaking down personality into four different types: Dominant & Driven; Influencing & Persuading; Secure & Steady; and Compliant & Considered.

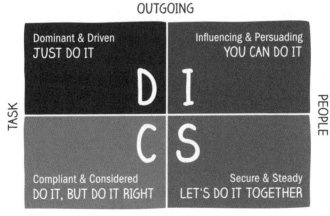

(Dr William Marston, 1929)

Broadly speaking, you will find developing a coaching mindset easier if you are people focused, therefore an I or S type rather than a more task-orientated D or C type. This is because you have a natural leaning towards collaborating with other people, whereas if you are task-orientated, your preference is for getting the job done. However, regardless of personality type, everyone can develop a coaching mindset – it's about being aware of one's own preference. Let's now look at each personality type in turn and examine how this can help or hinder you as you develop a coaching mindset.

D TYPE PERSONALITY: DOMINANT & DRIVEN

You are solution-orientated and results driven, so may find developing a 'pure' coaching mindset more challenging. You may feel frustrated waiting for the other person to discover their approach to solving a problem and be tempted to tell them how to do it instead. This preference lends itself well to mentoring and advising.

I TYPE PERSONALITY: INFLUENCING & PERSUADING

You are wired for people and like to inspire others, so are keen to help people improve. However, being outgoing, you will need to ensure that you remain objective and listen empathetically to the other person rather than tell them what you think they want to hear.

S TYPE PERSONALITY: SECURE & STEADY

You are reliable and people-orientated and will be naturally inclined to offer support and encouragement. However, you may find it difficult to adopt a mindset that challenges the other person, as you like to maintain the status quo.

C TYPE PERSONALITY: COMPLIANT & CONSIDERED

You are conscientious and thorough and will follow coaching procedures, frameworks and processes. However, you may struggle to be adaptable so that you can think in the moment during coaching conversations.

Having looked at each personality type in turn, it's important to recognize your own style. It's worth noting here that you may be a blend of two different personality types or more. Generally speaking, it is most common to be a blend D and C or I and S, as you are most likely to have a preference for *either* tasks *or* people.

Use the statements in the table on the next page to help you identify your most dominant style:

D TYPE PERSONALITY	I TYPE PERSONALITY	S TYPE PERSONALITY	C TYPE PERSONALITY
Confident & Results Driven	*Outgoing & Persuasive*	*Dependable & Consistent*	*Detail Orientated & Outcome Focused*
I am competitive and like to win	I focus on the big picture rather than detail	I'm a good listener	I am analytical and like to gather information
I am happy making decisions	Relationships are extremely important to me	I don't like confrontation	I do not like surprises
I like to be in control	I don't like to rock the boat	I consider other people's points of views	I don't show my emotions at work
I like to make things happen quickly	I like praise and recognition	I like to agree things by consensus	I don't like to rush decisions – I need all the facts

Whichever type or types you feel drawn to, try to value and respect the positives and take account of the limitations. If you are more task-orientated, you need to remind yourself of the benefits of coaching others and how this will make you feel. Whereas if you are wired for people, you are more likely to do this intuitively but will need to ensure you remain objective and listen to what the coachee has to say rather than offer advice.

Remember, as we said in the introduction – a manager needs to wear different hats and be a leader, trainer, mentor and coach. A **D type** personality will generally find it easy to lead and provide direction but more challenging to coach, whereas the opposite would be true of an **S type** personality who likes the security of making decisions as a team and finds it more difficult to be directive. The secret to being able to switch between these different roles is dialling up your emotional intelligence to help you get your head in the right place for the right type of conversation at the right time.

2. UNDERSTANDING YOURSELF ON A DEEPER LEVEL

Now that you have a basic understanding of your personality type and how this affects your mindset, it's time to dive deeper and work out exactly what makes you tick. So be brave, hold up a mirror and give yourself a full appraisal – the good, the bad and the ugly.

Self-knowledge is the cornerstone of emotional intelligence. You need to recognize and manage your emotions in order to understand and adapt to those of others. A great way to do this is to reflect on how you communicate on a good day and compare it to how you communicate on a bad day. Do you sometimes come across as overbearing or perhaps you don't assert yourself enough? Are you energetic, dynamic and charismatic or supportive, reassuring and encouraging? There are no right or wrong answers.

It's only by knowing your strengths and areas for development that you can understand the impact you have on others. The secret to developing a confident coaching mindset is accepting who you are and what you stand for and communicating this in an authentic manner. You need to practise what you preach and be true to the real you – otherwise you will lack credibility as a coach.

The next step to developing a coaching mindset is to draw on your self-reliance – another key emotional intelligence skill – and recognize that becoming a coach is a role that needs to be taken seriously. You are responsible for helping the coachee reach their full potential. This means trusting in your ability to judge and assess what support you think the coachee needs and not being unduly influenced by what they think they need. Your role is to be impartial and independent. You, therefore, need to draw on your self-control to think in the moment. This means being in tune with your emotions but staying calm and rational so that you can give the coachee your undivided attention.

Coaching and professional excellence author Tim Gallwey highlights the importance of being truly present in the moment in his book, *The Inner Game of Work*, where he argues that your Performance = your Potential – Interference.[2] In other words, you need to reduce the noise in your head (the interference) that prevents you from reaching your full potential in order to perform at your best.

As a coach, this noise is the worries and concerns that stop you from focusing on the other person. Perhaps you have too much on your plate and don't have the bandwidth to be able to listen attentively or maybe you feel intimidated by the person you are coaching. In either scenario, you need to recognize what is likely to cause you interference and take active steps to silence it.

3. RECOGNIZING YOUR SELF-LIMITING BELIEFS

We are all plagued with self-doubt from time to time. Even Michelle Obama has admitted to suffering from imposter syndrome – the fear of being discovered a fraud – when she said, "It doesn't go away, that feeling that you shouldn't take me that seriously. What do I know? I share that with you because we all have doubts in our abilities." These are the doubts or negative thoughts that can hold you back and undermine your coaching confidence. Perhaps you worry you don't have the necessary expertise to be an effective coach or you feel you lack the depth of experience to support other people. Below are four steps to help you banish these self-limiting beliefs so you can build a confident mindset.

SILENCE YOUR INNER GREMLIN

We're often our own worst enemies – talking ourselves down before we've even begun to coach. So, the next time you hear your inner gremlin – that negative voice inside your head – shouting in your ear, remember to turn the volume down by focusing instead on what's great about you, the work you do and your relationship with your team. By reminding yourself of your key strengths and achievements, you will reap the rewards of increased confidence.

MOVE OUT OF YOUR COMFORT ZONE

When your self-esteem takes a tumble, it becomes even harder to move out of your comfort zone. It's called a comfort zone for a reason – it's the place where you feel cosy and secure. However, it can also lead to negative emotions as it can cause you to shy away from new coaching opportunities. It is only by pushing your limits and moving into your stretch zone that you will learn and develop. So, face your fears and write a list of your main concerns and worries – e.g. "I'm too inexperienced to coach that person" and then think of a counter argument. Visualize what success looks like – whether it's someone you are coaching being promoted or learning a new skill. By picturing what good looks like, you are more likely to develop a coaching mindset that allows you to perform at your best.

DON'T BE A PERFECTIONIST

Setting exceptionally high coaching standards can ultimately lead to disappointment and demotivation. So, give yourself permission to make mistakes. Remember, a coach doesn't need to know all the answers, they just need to try and ask the right questions. Remind yourself that good is good enough and try not to judge yourself more harshly than you judge others.

ADOPT A POSITIVE OUTLOOK

You need to be optimistic and believe that coaching can help the person move forwards. By coaching the person to avoid thinking in black and white and to find the shades of grey, they are likely to see the positives in a situation and take the steps to reach their goals. This means drawing on your resilience to keep helping the other person find a solution that works for them.

Finally, a great way to overcome those self-limiting beliefs is to remind yourself of the satisfaction you will experience from watching the coachee go on a journey. This vocational pull will help counter your self-doubt and set you up for coaching success.

4. SHIFTING THE FOCUS FROM *ME* TO *THEM*

If we refer back to our definition of coaching as "helping the other person discover a new way forwards to fulfil their potential and maximize their performance," it becomes clear that developing a coaching mindset requires a shift in focus from 'me' to 'them'. Confident coaches understand that they need to empower their team, not micro manage them, for as the saying goes, "Give someone a fish and you feed them for a day, teach someone to fish and you feed them for a lifetime." This means helping your team with career development, expressing interest for your team members' success and personal wellbeing and having the necessary technical skills to be able to support them on their journey.

SHIFTING YOUR MINDSET

The table below shows how managers need to shift their mindsets when they begin a coaching conversation:

From
- Judgemental
- All knowing
- Directing
- Commanding & Controlling

To

- Objective
- Open-minded
- Facilitating
- Empowering & Encouraging

This takes adaptability – you need to be open to accepting that the coachee's view of reality may be different from your own and respond accordingly. It is not about deciding what *you* think is the best course of action, it's about helping *them* think for themselves.

EXERCISE

Complete the table below to help you understand the transition to a coaching mindset. Remember, it's about seeing things from the coachee's perspective. I have done the first two for you ...

FROM - YOU THINKING	TO - THEM THINKING
I know what your problem is	I know what the problem is
This is what you did wrong	I might do this differently
You need this support	...
These are your key strengths	...
Your self-doubt is holding you back	...
Your presentation needs work	...

Just like learning any new skill, shifting your mindset from *me* to *them* can be difficult to start with. However, the more you do it, the more confident you will become in your ability to adopt a rigorous and disciplined approach to coaching that focuses on the needs of the other person.

KEY TAKEAWAYS

By following the steps outlined in this section you will be well on your way to developing a coaching mindset that helps people reach their full potential. Coaching can seem daunting at first, so I always remind people that you don't have to be a great coach to get started, but you have to get started to be great coach. Be brave, curious and optimistic, and you will discover the immense satisfaction that comes from helping people be the best that they can be.

We've covered a lot of ground in this section, so here's a quick recap of the main points:

- Make it your priority to inspire and encourage your team members to be the best that they can be.
- Use the DISC model to identify your personality type and understand how this can help and hinder you as you develop a coaching mindset.
- Hold up a mirror and understand exactly what makes you tick so you can recognize and manage your own emotions during the coaching conversation.
- Be confident and accept who you are so you can communicate in an authentic and credible way.
- Take active steps to reduce the noise in your head, so you can focus on the needs of the coachee and perform at your best.
- Recognize the self-limiting beliefs that undermine your self-confidence and cause you to doubt your ability.
- Banish self-doubt by silencing your inner gremlin, moving out of your comfort zone, accepting that good is good enough and focusing on the positives.
- Shift the focus from *me* to *them*; this means being objective, open-minded, facilitating and empowering.

PART TWO

SETTING
YOURSELF UP
FOR COACHING
SUCCESS

Now that you have learned how to develop a coaching mindset, I want to share the practical tools and techniques that will help you set yourself up for coaching success. This is a key stage on the journey to becoming a confident coach as it helps to lay the groundwork for a successful coaching relationship. This will help you identify who and when to coach, how to coach for performance and how to contract effectively with the other person.

1. IDENTIFYING PEOPLE WHO NEED COACHING

Research by the Corporate Executive Board Company[3] shows that as a manager you are generally the best person to coach the members in your team. This is because you get to see your team in action on a daily basis and have the most opportunity to give constructive feedback in a timely way.

As mentioned in the Introduction, pure coaching alone is not enough to enable an individual to reach their full potential – they need a blended approach to learning and development. In my opinion, this is unfortunately where a lot of management and leadership systems get it wrong – there is no ONE way of doing things. As a manager, you have to constantly judge what is right for *that* individual at *that* time in order for you to give them the appropriate level of support. The Will and Skill Matrix (shown on the next page) is a powerful tool to help you consciously decide the best learning approach to adopt. This management tool was made popular by Max Landsberg's book, *The Tao of Coaching* (1996).

The Will and Skill Matrix

Let's start by defining exactly what we mean by will and skill. Will is the coachee's attitude, motivation and level of confidence, whereas skill is their capability, knowledge and experience. This is not cast in stone – the same person may have different levels of will and skill according to the particular task or situation they find themselves in. For example, a person could have high skill and high will when it comes to managing projects on time but low skill and low will when it comes to presenting to their customers. So, always plot where individuals sit on the matrix relative to a particular situation or problem they are trying to overcome.

As the matrix shows, when a person has high will but low skill, training is generally the most appropriate approach as they are self-motivated but may need to be taught new skills. If, however, a person has low will and low skill, they may need a more directive approach and have to be managed on a day-to-day basis until their will and skill increase.

With someone who has high skill but low will, a development coaching approach is a powerful way to help understand what may be causing their low will and inspire them to go the extra mile.

Finally, if someone has high will and high skill, they are generally an ideal person to performance coach – they have the desire to improve and build on their strengths and are more likely to take ownership of their own development and recognize ways in which they can raise the bar so they can reach their full potential.

Bear in mind that where an individual sits on the Will and Skill Matrix will change over time. For example, if someone new joins your team, you may need to train them in order to get them up to speed, whereas once they have been working in a role for a long time, they may need coaching to help them set new goals. It's important to define will and skill relative to the specific individual – not as they compare to other people. And remember to focus on the individual's potential as well as their current performance.

Another great tool for identifying when people would benefit from coaching, training or from being managed more closely is the Johari Window. This is a personal development technique developed by a team of psychologists in the 1950s.

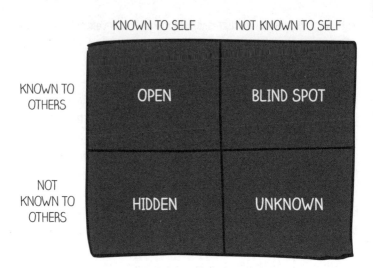

	KNOWN TO SELF	NOT KNOWN TO SELF
KNOWN TO OTHERS	OPEN	BLIND SPOT
NOT KNOWN TO OTHERS	HIDDEN	UNKNOWN

The Johari Window
(Luft and Harrington, 1955)

Look at the window from the perspective of the person you are going to coach:

- The OPEN box shows what is known to others as well as themselves. This could be their level of technical expertise or strengths they are proud of.
- The BLIND SPOT is what is known to others but not known to themselves. Perhaps they don't understand the impact they are having on other people in their team or are over-confident but haven't yet earned their stripes.
- The UNKNOWN box is what is not known to others or to themselves. This could be their full potential – perhaps they haven't yet been fully tested or given the opportunity to be the best that they can be.

- The HIDDEN box is what is not known to others but is known to themselves. This can be where self-doubt and imposter syndrome lurk – self-limiting beliefs about their ability that they are reluctant to share with others.

As a coach, you need to harness your emotional intelligence to judge whether members of your team have any blind spots or hidden concerns that could be helped with coaching. This takes awareness, curiosity and empathy on your part. Don't be tempted to make a snap judgement – whenever possible, gather feedback to ensure you have a balanced view.

By using the Will and Skill Matrix combined with the Johari Window, you can confidently identify what people need to reduce blind spots, banish self-limiting beliefs and develop new skills that enable them to reach their full potential.

2. COACHING FOR INCREASED PERFORMANCE

Once you've identified who you want to coach and what they need help with, you need to set the appropriate level of challenge to enable the person to improve their performance. After all, what doesn't challenge us, doesn't change us. The graph below shows the critical role that challenge plays in driving performance.

PERFORMANCE

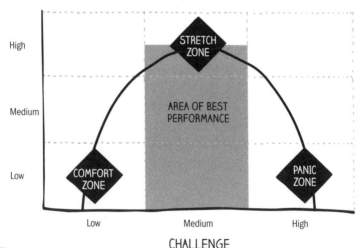

The vertical axis shows the individual's performance levels and the horizontal axis reflects how challenged that person is feeling. The graph shows that an individual performs at their best when they experience a medium level of challenge. This is the area of best performance. Your role as a coach is to challenge the person to move out of their comfort zone and into their stretch zone so they can learn and develop. However, you have to use your judgement to ensure you don't tip them into the panic zone where their performance would dip once again.

Helping people move out of their comfort zone can be easier said than done – it's the place where people feel safe and secure. However, it can also cause them to shy away from trying something new or leave them feeling complacent and stuck in a rut. If you have noticed that someone on your team feels bored, demotivated and easily distracted they may well be stuck in their comfort zone. Your role as their coach is to follow the steps below to help them move into their stretch zone.

HOW TO HELP PEOPLE MOVE INTO THEIR AREA OF BEST PERFORMANCE

1. **Get them to face their fears** – help them to list their main concerns, then ask them to think of a counter argument.
   An example could be:
   "I'm terrified of speaking in public"
   With the possible counter argument:
   "I presented my slides with confidence at the last team meeting."

By coaching them to flip these negative thoughts or beliefs into positives, they will reap the reward of improved confidence that will boost their performance.

2. **Make a plan** – take practical steps to put an action plan together that propels them out of their comfort zone so they can move forwards and grow.

3. **Break their down goals into bite-size chunks** – Remind them that they don't need to move into their stretch zone with one giant leap. As the saying goes, "How do you eat an elephant?... In bite-sized chunks!" So, in the case of someone who has a fear of public speaking, coach them to consider ideas like hosting a webinar or speaking on a panel as opposed to volunteering to be the keynote speaker at an industry-wide summit.

4. **Inspire them to raise their game** – Ask them to think of people they admire. What would they do in this situation?

A word of caution: while helping the person move into their stretch zone will boost confidence and improve their performance, a move into their panic zone can leave them feeling stressed and out of their depth.

It is important when conducting these types of coaching conversations that you enable them to articulate *their* thoughts, ideas and actions rather than giving them suggestions. More on how to do this in Part 3.

You can ensure that the **level of challenge is appropriate by looking out for the following signs**. If displayed, any one of these could indicate they have moved into their panic zone:

1. They are easily overwhelmed and struggle to focus.
2. They find it difficult to make a decision.
3. They are tired and look worried.
4. They suffer from tension headaches or complain of stomach troubles.
5. They view constructive feedback as personal criticism.

It's important for you to use your judgement to offer the appropriate level of support and challenge, depending on where the person is on their performance journey. The diagram below illustrates this:

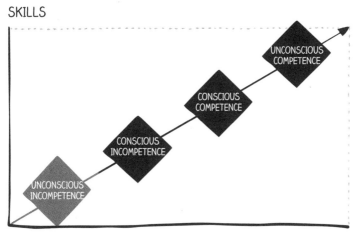

SKILLS

UNCONSCIOUS COMPETENCE

CONSCIOUS COMPETENCE

CONSCIOUS INCOMPETENCE

UNCONSCIOUS INCOMPETENCE

TRAINING

People in need of coaching usually start their journey with **unconscious incompetence** – this is their blind spot – an area for development they don't know they have. They may require a high level of challenge to move out of their comfort zone and become **consciously incompetent** – where they recognize gaps in their knowledge and/or the self-limiting beliefs they have kept hidden. Stage three is **conscious competence**, here they have well and truly entered their stretch zone and are working hard to consciously change their behaviour and develop new skills. The final stage in the journey to optimal performance is **unconscious competence** when their new skills and behaviour are firmly embedded and feel like second nature. At this stage, the level of challenge drops again, and you can give yourself a well-earned pat on the back – your job as a coach is done for the moment!

3. CONTRACTING FORMALLY VS. INFORMALLY

A final but important action required to position coaching for success is to contract effectively with the coachee. Contracting is the process of establishing a shared understanding between the coach and the coachee about what will take place during the coaching relationship. In its simplest terms, it's an agreement about how you are both going to work together and, as such, it needs to be done from the outset as it will lay the foundation for the coaching relationship going forwards.

If you are coaching in a formal setting – e.g. via a third party – you will generally need to provide a written document that details the coaching boundaries, guidelines and code of ethics. However, it's just as important to use a contract when you are coaching in an informal situation; for example, if as a manager you are coaching your team. In this kind of situation, you need to ensure you convey professionalism by agreeing on how often you will meet, when and where. By setting and noting your expectations of the coachee, and formalizing their expectations of you, you will ensure there is no ambiguity or confusion later.

Examples of coaching expectations:

EXPECTATIONS OF THE COACH	EXPECTATIONS OF THE COACHEE
Turn up on time	Turn up on time
Set the appropriate level of challenge	Come to the sessions prepared
Manage the coaching process	Complete follow-up actions
Support, not provide answers	Drive the content of the coaching sessions
Respect the coachee's point of view	Respect the coach's point of view
Be trustworthy and confidential	Have honest and open conversations

A manager will need to wear different hats when training, managing, mentoring or coaching, so it's particularly important to establish absolute clarity about coaching expectations. For example, don't be tempted to use your coaching one-to-ones as business updates and forget that the focus should be their personal development. The other person needs to know that when you are in coaching mode, you will not provide them with the answers you would give them as a manager, trainer or mentor. Without the coaching contract, the other person might get confused about when you are supporting them and when you are telling them what they need to do.

Confidentiality is critical and lies at the heart of coaching contracting. As a manager, you need to ensure you are impartial and respect the coachee's point of view. This is key to building trust. So, if you feel there is a conflict of interest – for example, internal politics among your team – you need to put your hand up and find someone else to coach the person instead. This way you are behaving ethically and ensuring that the pathway is clear for the other person to reach their full potential.

KEY TAKEAWAYS

There are lots of great tools and techniques in this section to help you position coaching for success. Here's a quick refresher:

- Adopt a blended and disciplined approach to coaching that enables you to offer the appropriate level of support to the right person at the right time.
- Use the Will and Skill Matrix to help identify the optimal time to train, manage or coach someone.
- The Johari Window is an invaluable technique to help uncover a coachee's blind spots and hidden concerns.
- What doesn't challenge us, doesn't change us – use your emotional intelligence to recognize when people in your team are bored, demotivated and stuck in their comfort zones.
- Help the coachee move out of their comfort zone and into their stretch zone – their area of best performance.
- Use the performance pathway to set the appropriate level of challenge as the coachee moves from unconscious incompetence to unconscious competence.
- Whether you are coaching formally or informally, articulate your coaching boundaries, guidelines and code of ethics. These will lay the foundations for a successful coaching relationship going forwards.
- To avoid any ambiguity or confusion, from the beginning clarify your expectations as a coach and expectations of the coachee from you.
- Confidentiality lies at the heart of contracting – so make sure you are impartial and respect the other person's point of view.

PART THREE

ADOPTING A DISCIPLINED APPROACH

Once you have successfully contracted with the other person – either formally or informally – it's time to get to the crux of the matter and begin the coaching conversation. This is the moment when your coaching confidence needs to be rock solid.

Coaching is, in essence, about asking the right question in the right way at the right time and *listening* with emotional intelligence to the response. Although this can seem daunting at first, it's entirely normal to feel unsure about what questions you are going to ask and how you are going to structure the coaching conversation.

The great news is that there is a tried and tested framework you can use to help the coachee set goals and solve problems so that they can unlock their full potential. By drawing on your self-control (a key emotional intelligence skill) and adopting a disciplined approach to coaching, you will soon find that your confidence increases as you begin to ask questions in a methodical and engaging way.

1. INTRODUCING THE GROW FRAMEWORK

The GROW model is a well-established coaching framework that was originally developed in the 1980s by business coaches Graham Alexander, Alan Fine and Sir John Whitmore. It is a simple but extremely powerful tool that helps structure the coaching conversation into four stages and is widely acknowledged as coaching best practice.

| GOAL | REALITY | OPTIONS | WILL ACTION |

Let's start by taking a top-line view of the model before working through each of the four stages in greater detail.

GOAL

The purpose of this stage is to help the person work out what they want to achieve through their coaching session or sessions. This could be overcoming a particular challenge they are facing or setting a new target they want to reach. As a coach, you need to ensure the goals they set are SMART: specific, measurable, ambitious, relevant and timed.

For example, for someone who wants to improve their negotiation skills, a SMART goal would be: "I want to be able to balance the playing field when I negotiate with key customers so I am on an equal footing [specific]. My aim is to agree on the new contract, negotiate an appropriately ambitious price for my products and demonstrate the value I can bring to the table [measurable and ambitious]. I need to develop this skill ahead of next month's sales meeting with them [timed]."

It's important not to rush this stage as it frames the rest of the conversation. By taking the time to help the coachee identify and set SMART goals – either short or long term – you enable them to see the wood for the trees and gain clarity and focus.

REALITY

The next stage is to help them assess the reality of the situation in the context of the goal that has been set. It's important to remember to concentrate on *their* reality – not how *you* view the situation. Your role as coach is to help the person stop and think, then to encourage them to look at the situation from as many angles as possible so they can get to the bottom of what is really going on. Without this stage, they are in danger of treating the symptoms instead of discovering the root cause of the problem.

It is so important, as their coach, to remain impartial, resisting the temptation to influence their version of the reality.

OPTIONS

Now that you both have a clear picture of what is going on, you need to help the coachee discover how to fix the situation. Encourage them to be creative and brainstorm ideas that can help them move towards the goal they have set themselves. The aim of this stage is to get them to explore as many options as possible so they can discover a solution that works for them.

WILL ACTION

The final stage in the GROW model is to help the coachee clarify what they will do next and to have a clear plan of action. It's vital that they identify how they are going to hold themselves to account so that they take full responsibility for actioning these next steps.

Although the GROW model appears very linear when written down in this way, in reality coaching conversations tend to be more fluid. The other person may need to revisit some of the stages during the coaching sessions to help them gain greater clarity and stay motivated. So, resist the temptation to stick rigidly to the framework and use it as a guiding principle instead.

2. DEVELOPING YOUR QUESTIONING TECHNIQUE

Now that you have a better understanding of the four stages in the GROW model, it's time to look at how to hone your questioning technique so that you know which questions to ask when.

Broadly speaking, there are two types of questions: open questions that start with *Who? When? How?* and *What?* and closed questions beginning with *Is? Was?* and *Did?* Both types of question are relevant in a coaching conversation; however, it's important to recognize that they drive different responses.

Open questions should be used to help you gather information and encourage the other person to open up, as they require a descriptive answer. Commonly used examples could be, "How did you feel that meeting went?", "What do you think was good about your report?" or "Describe how you feel about your feedback."

Closed questions, on the other hand, are useful for clarifying facts and confirming details as they drive a "yes" or "no" response. Examples include, "Does this make sense?", "Have you understood this situation correctly?" and "Are you surprised by this feedback?"

As a coach, you need to use your judgement to decide which type of question is most appropriate at a given time. For example, asking a closed question such as, "Are there any barriers preventing you reaching your goal?" in the reality stage might close down the conversation, whereas asking, "What barriers are preventing you from reaching your goal?" encourages the other person to dig deeper.

I also generally advise against using the question *why* when you are coaching. This is because it can be seen as a leading question or imply that you are judging the other person, even though this might not be your intention.

EXERCISE

Here's the scenario:

A newly promoted direct report has come to you to say they are struggling with their bigger role and feeling stressed and upset.

Now convert the following closed or leading questions into open questions that allow you to explore the reality of the situation. I have done the first couple for you to illustrate the difference.

Do you feel stressed all the time?	How often are you feeling really stressed?
Why don't you de-prioritize the less urgent things off your list?	How could you prioritize your workload so you feel calmer?

Do you need some time off?	...
Are there any barriers stopping you dealing with this stress?	...
Has this discussion helped you?	...

Let's now refer back to the GROW model and apply our questioning techniques to the four stages to help establish a clear direction during the conversation. I have included an example scenario at the end of each stage to help bring the GROW model to life. Remember, not every question will be applicable to each coaching conversation you have, so use them as a guide to structure your conversation, rather than religiously asking each one in turn.

STAGE ONE: GOAL

Your aim is to help the other person define their short- or long-term goals and clarify what they want to achieve through the coaching sessions by asking the following questions:

- *What topic or issue would you like to discuss?*
- *What does success look like?*
- *How do you measure success?*
- *What specifically would you like to have achieved by the end of the session?*
- *What will be the impact of achieving this goal/not achieving this goal?*
- *How challenging or exciting is this goal?*
- *What control do you have of this goal?*

Watch out: Sometimes the coachee might struggle to understand what they want to get out of the coaching conversation. So, don't get too hung up on identifying exactly what the goal is, as this can stop you moving the conversation forwards. Instead, move on to the reality stage to help them gain greater insight into their current situation before finalizing their goal.

Example scenario
Your coachee is feeling demotivated and frustrated because they do not feel that they are being challenged enough. After answering these questions, they define their GOAL as wanting to be promoted within the next 12 months.

STAGE TWO: REALITY
By asking the following types of questions, you encourage the coachee to explore the situation fully before they start to come up with solutions:

- *What is going on right now that tells you that you have an issue?*
- *What has brought this to a head?*
- *What have you done so far to achieve this goal?*
- *What were the results from following these steps?*
- *What resources do you have to help you achieve your outcome?*
- *What other resources do you need?*
- *What barriers are currently stopping you from moving forwards?*

Watch out: It can be tempting for both parties to rush this stage and move on to trying to solve the actual problem. So, try to avoid being too high level and take the time to help the other person dive deeper and assess the reality of the situation. If appropriate, don't forget to praise them for the progress they have made so far.

Example scenario

By exploring their current situation, your coachee will identify where they lack some of the technical skills necessary to be promoted to the next level of responsibility in the organization. They also recognize that their self-doubt has been holding them back and preventing them from taking the next step in their career.

STAGE THREE: OPTIONS

You need to work with the other person to brainstorm as many options as possible. Remember, it's their responsibility to come up with the ideas, not yours. Here are the types of questions that can help them:

- *What could you do just now to move you one step nearer to your goal?*
- *If there were no barriers to success, what would you do?*
- *If you secretly knew what you should do first, what would it be?*
- *What else could you do?*
- *If you went to a colleague with this, what might they suggest?*
- *If you look back at your list, do any points spark another idea?*

Watch out: Don't forget to reserve judgement. Brainstorm rules apply – no idea is a bad idea. Your aim is to encourage the coachee to think creatively so that they maintain responsibility for their ideas.

Example scenario

Through brainstorming, your coachee creates a list of ideas that include: finding a mentor, signing up for a training course, taking on greater responsibility in their role, attending networking events, transferring to a different company and applying for a new role.

STEP FOUR: WILL ACTION

Set the coachee up for success by checking their commitment level and helping them agree to specific actions and timeframes using the following questions:

- *Out of all these options, what are you going to do?*
- *How will these actions meet your main goal?*
- *When are you going to take these actions?*
- *Does anyone else need to be involved?*
- *What involvement do you need from them?*
- *How committed do you feel on a scale of one to ten?*
- *Can you think of any barrier that might stop you from doing it?*
- *How are you going to overcome that barrier?*

Watch out: Don't burden yourself with the coachee's actions. Make sure you stand back and let them take control of their plan of action.

Example scenario

Your coachee has agreed to sign up for a training course by the beginning of September to hone the technical skills required for the promotion. They have also committed to identifying and attending one networking event per month to help build their personal brand and boost their self-confidence so that they are in the best possible position to secure their promotion in 12 months' time.

3. BUILDING A BANK OF BEST PRACTICE COACHING QUESTIONS

You should now have a clear understanding of the best way to structure the coaching conversation and the types of questions you need to ask. It's therefore time to put the theory into practice and begin coaching people. The more coaching conversations you have, the more confident you will become in your ability to ask the right questions at the right time. Use the table on the opposite page to help build up a bank of questions that you feel have worked particularly well in the different stages of the GROW model to help you embed your learning.

Like learning any new skill, when it comes to asking questions, practice really does make perfect. Once you have gained some experience, you will be ready to move on to the more advanced questioning techniques outlined below.

GOAL

...

...

...

▼

REALITY

...

...

...

▼

OPTIONS

...

...

...

▼

WILL ACTION

...

...

...

SIX ADVANCED QUESTIONING TECHNIQUES

Take your questioning technique to the next level by incorporating the following types of questions into your coaching conversations. I have included a tick box before each question so that you can check them off when you have used them successfully in a coaching session.

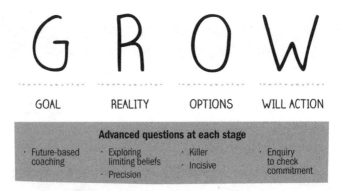

Advanced questions at each stage			
· Future-based coaching	· Exploring limiting beliefs · Precision	· Killer · Incisive	· Enquiry to check commitment

1. Asking future-based questions

These types of questions are particularly applicable to the GOAL stage of the GROW model, as they encourage the other person to look forwards and help them articulate what good looks like:

> *What do you hope to gain from our conversation today?*
> *How will you know if it has been useful?*
> *What do you really want to happen?*
> *What would good look like?*

2. Using questions to explore self-limiting beliefs

During the REALITY stage, it's important to explore any self-limiting beliefs that may be holding the other person back. Your aim is to ask the following types of questions to challenge their negative thoughts and help them see the reality of the situation:

What do you think is stopping you?
What beliefs do you need to change for you to progress?
What would happen if you did/did not ... ?

3. Asking precision questions

Precision questions allow you to probe further into what the other person is saying. They are extremely useful in the REALITY stage as they allow you to challenge what has been said and help you expose generalizations and comparisons to help the other person better understand how they feel:

What, always?
Says who?
Better than whom?
What specifically?

4. Using killer questions

As the name suggests, killer questions should be used sparingly to stay effective and are most applicable in the OPTIONS stage. They are useful if the other person is feeling stuck, as they can challenge them to think differently and come up with new ideas:

What is the question you want me to ask you?
If you knew the answer, what would it be?
If you could do anything without consequence, what would you do?

5. Asking incisive questions

These are questions that focus on the 'what-ifs' by helping suspend any self-limiting beliefs. They are a powerful way to foster creativity and are therefore very useful in the OPTIONS stage when you are encouraging the other person to brainstorm different ideas:

What would you do if there was not a problem?
What advice would you give to a colleague facing the same challenge?
What is the maddest/hardest/easiest/silliest thing you could do?

6. Using enquiry questions

Enquiry questions are used to check the other person's commitment levels and for this reason come to the fore in the WILL ACTION stage. They are a great way to ensure that the coachee has taken responsibility for their actions and are completing their next steps:

Based on today's conversation, when will you reflect on x?
On a scale of one to ten, how likely are you to action x?
When are you going to do x?

Finally, I want to share a very effective questioning technique that helps when managing work stress levels. Unfortunately, with the rise of workplace stress, it is important and necessary to be aware of these types of questions as you are likely to have many opportunities to use them.

So, if you notice someone in your team appearing visibly stressed, engage in conversation by asking them:

"What will happen if you stay stressed?"

Answers could include lack of sleep, long hours at work and/or worsening relationships at home. I then follow this with the question:

"What won't happen if you stay stressed?"

This often triggers responses such as:

"I won't be able to achieve what I want to achieve"

or

"I won't be able to balance work and personal life."

I finish with the question:

"What will happen if you are not stressed?"

To which they often reply that their energy levels will return, they will feel more in control and be back to their old self.

By asking these three questions, you are helping them recognize the symptoms of stress and the effect it is having on their body and mind. You are also encouraging them to visualize what good looks like to help them take positive steps to change their behaviour and reduce their stress levels.

4. LEARNING HOW TO LISTEN WITH EMOTIONAL INTELLIGENCE

Having developed your questioning technique, next it's crucial to draw on your emotional intelligence and listen carefully to the coachee's responses. This may sound obvious, but all too often, people confuse hearing with listening; hearing is an involuntary, physiological process involving your ears, whereas listening is a learned skill and mental process that uses your body and mind. The diagram below shows the three different levels of listening:

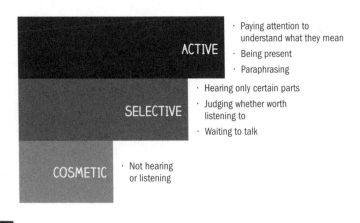

ACTIVE
- Paying attention to understand what they mean
- Being present
- Paraphrasing

SELECTIVE
- Hearing only certain parts
- Judging whether worth listening to
- Waiting to talk

COSMETIC
- Not hearing or listening

Cosmetic listening – when you are pretending to listen but are actually thinking about something else entirely. Perhaps you are worrying about a looming deadline and find it hard to concentrate on your coaching one-to-one.

Selective listening – when you only listen to what you want to hear. This could be because your judgement gets in the way or you are too busy waiting to talk to focus on what the other person has to say. An all-too-common mistake.

Active listening – when you draw on emotional intelligence to listen in the moment so you can process exactly what the other person is saying and see things from their perspective.

Confident coaches recognize that they need to harness their empathy to listen to what the other person is saying so they can understand things from their point of view. By giving the other person your undivided attention, you are making them feel valued and important. This will help you build trust in the long term. I'm sure all of us can think of a time when we haven't been listened to properly and how this has made us feel. So, follow the five steps on the next page to help you become an active listener.

FIVE STEPS TO EFFECTIVE ACTIVE LISTENING

1. **Be really 'present'** – calm your mind and focus on the person in front of you by minimizing any interference in your head.

2. **Ask questions to understand, not to be understood** – as Stephen Covey explains in his seminal book *The Seven Habits of Highly Effective People*, you need to focus on what the other person has to say rather than on what you want to communicate.

3. **Be aware of barriers that hinder your listening** – these can be the self-limiting beliefs or impartiality we covered in Part One.

4. **Stay focused** – remember, listening is an active process and takes effort so try to ensure your attention doesn't wander.

5. **Capture and check the message** – summarizing reassures the other person that you have listened carefully to them and, most importantly, understood what they are trying to say.

Developing your listening skills takes hard work and commitment, so challenge yourself to actively listen to other people on a daily basis – whether it's listening to a colleague in a meeting or when you are catching up with your friends or family at home. I will cover listening in greater detail in the next section when I look at the importance of reading beyond the words.

By following the GROW model, drawing on the bank of questions outlined and harnessing your emotional intelligence to listen with empathy, you will have the tools and techniques at your fingertips to help you on your journey to becoming a confident coach. But, it's important to understand that learning to become a coach is difficult, and it can take approximately 250 hours to qualify as a professional coach.

KEY TAKEAWAYS

I hope this section has helped allay some of your fears about starting and structuring a coaching conversation. Here's a quick reminder of the main points I've covered to help you on your way:

- Coaching is about asking the right questions at the right time and listening with emotional intelligence to the answers.
- Follow the GROW model, a tried and tested framework to help you structure your coaching conversation.
- Use the GOAL stage to help the coachee define what they want to achieve through the sessions.
- Build a picture of the situation in the context of the goal during the REALITY stage.
- Encourage the coachee to brainstorm ideas to help them solve their problem in the OPTIONS stage.
- Help the coachee agree on specific actions and timeframes in the WILL ACTION stage.
- Hone your questioning technique by using both open and closed questions to help the coachee move towards their goal.
- Use open questions to help gather information and closed questions to confirm details.
- Refer to the bank of example questions and learn which to ask in each of the four stages of the GROW model.
- Put theory into practice – the more coaching you do, the more confident you will become at asking the right questions at the right time.

- Take your questioning technique to the next level by including:
  - Future-based questions
  - Questions that explore self-limiting beliefs
  - Incisive questions
  - Killer questions
  - Enquiry questions

- Support people in your team who appear visibly stressed by asking them:
  - *"What will happen if you stay stressed?"*
  - *"What won't happen if you stay stressed?"*
  - *"What will happen if you are not stressed?"*

- Take practical steps to become an active listener by drawing on your empathy to listen in the moment and see things from the coachee's perspective.

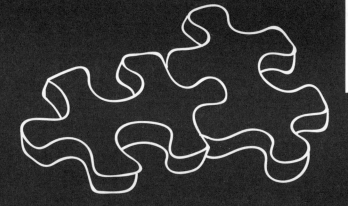

PART FOUR

MANAGING YOURSELF DURING THE COACHING CONVERSATION

With a clear understanding of the GROW model and a bank of questions that will help you structure your coaching sessions, it's time to focus on the challenging task of managing yourself during the coaching conversation itself. This is where the magic happens, so it is important to focus on this.

The secret to becoming a great coach is to leverage your emotional intelligence so you are able to think in the moment while using your social skills to start building a relationship with the other person. I often compare this to learning to drive a car; it sounds easy in theory but is hard to do in practice.

Throughout this section, I'll show you how to be truly present, help you handle different personality types, enable you to listen beyond the words and share practical steps to build trust and rapport. Let's refer back to the emotional intelligence diagram to better understand the skills you need to focus on during the coaching conversation.

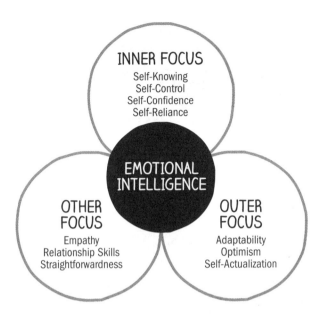

Inner focus: Draw on your self-knowledge to understand the impact you are having on the coachee, your self-control to be truly present in the moment, your self-confidence to silence any self-doubt and your self-reliance to believe you have the tools and techniques at your fingertips to help your coachee be the best that they can be.

Other focus: Harness your empathy to put yourself in the coachee's shoes, your relationship skills to build trust and rapport and your straightforwardness to have an honest and open conversation.

Outer focus: Be agile so you can adapt to different personality types and remain optimistic, believing that a solution can be found. It's only by combining these core emotional intelligence skills that you can move from good to great and become a coach who successfully manages and controls the coaching conversation.

1. BEING TRULY PRESENT IN THE MOMENT

Here it's worth referring back to Part One on developing a coaching mindset to remind yourself of Tim Gallwey's definition of performance being the sum of potential minus interference (page 20). Your role as a coach is to reduce the amount of interference in your own head and the head of your coachee so that you are both able to be truly present during the coaching sessions. When you first start to coach someone, the potential for interference can be considerable. The six different dialogues outlined below illustrate the levels of interference that can occur and how this can limit both parties' ability to process what is being said during the coaching conversation itself.

SIX DIALOGUES THAT CREATE INTERFERENCE

1. Your inner dialogue before the conversation
Imagine you are about to coach someone for the first time. Before you even sit down with them, chances are your brain will start to consider how the conversation will go:

- *"I wonder if they'll show up on time?"*
- *"What will happen if there's no chemistry?"*
- *"I'm not looking forward to giving them some difficult feedback."*

2. Your coachee's inner dialogue before the conversation

It's entirely normal for your coachee to feel apprehensive about their upcoming coaching session with thoughts such as:

- *"I don't like being put on the spot."*
- *"What if I'm asked to talk about something that I don't want to share?"*
- *"I haven't finished my actions from the last session."*

3. Your inner dialogue during the conversation

This is the voice in your head speaking to you during the coaching session itself. Perhaps you feel you didn't pitch a particular question the right way or you are not feeling as though rapport is building:

- *"They clearly didn't like the last question I asked."*
- *"They don't seem very engaged."*
- *"I can't believe they haven't done their preparation."*

4. Your coachee's inner dialogue during the conversation

At the same time, the other person will have thoughts running through their mind during their coaching one-to-one. They could be feeling frustrated:

- *"I just want to be told the answer."*
- *"I really can't come up with any new ideas."*
- *"I really don't want to be given any extra work to do."*

5. Your reflections after the conversation

After you have finished the session, you are likely to start reviewing your performance:

- *"I feel like we ended on the wrong note."*
- *"I wasn't as impartial as I'd planned to be."*
- *"I'm not sure they've taken full responsibility for their actions."*

6. Your coachee's reflections after the conversation

The other person is also likely to question their part in the conversation. For example, they could be worrying about what they have revealed to you:

- *"I hope I didn't open up too much."*
- *"I'm concerned they will see me in a different light."*
- *"I've committed to a plan of action, but how am I going to find the time to do it?"*

The six examples above demonstrate how internal dialogue can compete for attention with the spoken word during the conversations in a coaching session. As a coach, you need to be fully aware of this interference and take practical steps to try to reduce it. This is the reason that your preparation is so important. As a coach, you are completely in control of this. Preparation really is everything, especially as you start on your journey to becoming a confident coach. So, use your self-knowledge to identify what distracts you when you go into a coaching session. For example, if you are a visual person, perhaps the hustle and bustle of an office will prevent you from being truly present. In which case, try and sit somewhere that doesn't have other people in your line of sight so you can give your coachee your full attention. Or if you know that you find it difficult to resist checking your phone from time to time, consciously leave it in your bag or pocket so that you are less likely to be distracted by it.

It's all about getting your head in the right place so you are ready to give the other person your undivided attention. Personally, I always begin a new coaching session by turning to a clean page in my notebook and writing down the name of the person I am coaching and the date. The physical action of doing this steadies my mind and acts as a signal for me to clear my mind and dial down the noise that may be going on in my brain, so that I am ready to start the coaching conversation.

EXERCISE

Take a moment to fill in the table below to work out what you should start doing to help you be present, what you should stop doing that causes you interference and what you should continue to do to stay focused on the other person's needs.

START	STOP	CONTINUE
...	...	...
...	...	...
...	...	...

Once you have taken active steps to reduce the interference on your part, you need to think about how to help the other person be present in the moment. If, for example, the person you are about to coach is an introverted person who struggles to open up, you could suggest meeting in a private meeting room where they will feel more comfortable discussing their feelings. The greater your understanding of the coachee and what makes them tick, the better you will be at minimizing any interference. This takes me nicely to the importance of learning how to recognize and respond to different personality types.

2. HANDLING DIFFERENT PERSONALITY TYPES

You should already have a fairly clear idea of your dominant personality type based on the statements you selected from the table of DISC personality type descriptions in Part 1. The secret to managing yourself in the moment is to draw on your awareness to identify the personality type of the person you are coaching. Your ability to recognize and then handle these different personality types is crucial to building a successful coaching relationship. The DISC diagram is included again here to help remind you of the four different personality types.

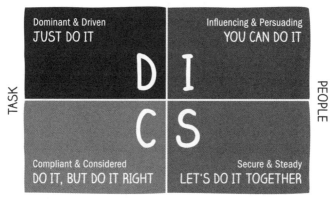

(Dr William Marston, 1929)

Below is a brief explanation of the most common types of behaviour displayed by the four personality types to help identify their dominant personality type and what a coach may need to watch out for.

D TYPES

As dominant and driven individuals, they are likely to be punctual, determined and purposeful. D types will commit to their coaching sessions as they are the type that is keen to improve their performance and be successful.

Watch out: D types will be impatient for results and won't want the coaching process to take too much time. They are more likely to interrupt you and try to take control of the conversation. This may mean that they are less likely to listen carefully to the questions you are asking them.

I TYPES

As people who love to influence and persuade, they will be enthusiastic, warm and animated. They will enjoy the chit-chat and be happy to discuss their feelings.

Watch out: I types often lack focus and attention when it comes to details. They are likely to adopt a hasty approach and be reluctant to go through the methodology. Instead, they generally prefer to rush to the REALITY stage.

S TYPES

As secure and steady individuals, they will be good at listening and accepting of the coaching framework. S types will ask lots of questions to help them understand. They are patient and won't expect to see immediate results.

Watch out: S types prefer to maintain the status quo, so are most likely to struggle with the OPTIONS stage because they don't like change. They don't like to be challenged so are more likely to come up with a list of conservative ideas. They are often sensitive, so may take feedback personally.

C TYPES

As compliant and considered individuals, they will take coaching extremely seriously – turning up on time having done all their preparation. They like to follow rules and procedures and will analyse and question every aspect of the coaching process.

Watch out: C types can be hard to read as they don't like to show their feelings. They are often perfectionists, so may worry about making changes unless there's proof that a course of action has worked. They tend to ask lots of questions which can make it a challenge to keep the conversation moving forwards.

TOP TIPS ON HANDLING DIFFERENT PERSONALITY TYPES

Once you have read and interpreted the coachee's personality type, you need to be agile and adaptable to flex your coaching style and manage the conversation effectively. For example, if you are both

D type personalities, make sure the conversation doesn't turn into a power battle. Instead, draw on your self-control to slow down the pace so they have time to think about the questions you are asking. If, on the other hand, you are coaching a person with an I type personality, ensure they stick to the model and do not go off on a tangent. Also, although I type personalities are good at looking at the big picture, you will need to challenge them to complete their actions since they tend to struggle with the detail. When it comes to S type personalities, generally they are quite sensitive and likely to take feedback to heart and view it as a criticism, so you need to be careful about how you give them feedback. Finally, when it comes to coaching C type personalities, make sure you are fully prepared by gathering evidence to support the coaching sessions. They will need to see facts and figures to help them decide what is the right course of action for them.

A handy technique that helps you manage all four different personality types is the power of silence. If you consciously stay quiet during the coaching conversation, you may be amazed by the other person's response. As well as giving yourself valuable thinking time, it can help slow down the pace of the conversation and allow the coachee time to reflect. This can help them process their thoughts. This period of silence doesn't have to last longer than 30 seconds for it to be extremely effective. However, it can feel like forever the first time you do it, so it's important to hold your nerve and feel comfortable with it.

Silence is a very powerful technique when used in the first three stages of the GROW model as it enables the coachee to do most of the talking and helps transfer responsibility over to them. Like any communication technique, you need to vary how often you use it and choose the most appropriate situations to put it into practice.

3. LISTENING BEYOND THE WORDS

In the last section, we looked at the importance of harnessing empathy to actively listen to the other person. You now need to take this a step further and develop the ability to listen beyond their words. This is because only 7% of what we communicate comes from our spoken words, 38% comes from our tone of voice and 55% comes from non-verbal cues such as our body language.[4]

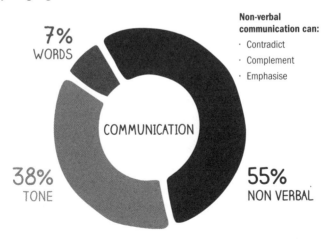

Non-verbal communication can:
· Contradict
· Complement
· Emphasise

7%
WORDS

COMMUNICATION

38%
TONE

55%
NON VERBAL

Communication is more than the words you say

By using self-control to be present in the moment, you will be able to focus on reading the coachee's body language and identify whether it is complementing, contradicting or emphasizing what they are saying. For example, if the coachee tells you they are keen to hear feedback, then leans back with their arms folded waiting for your comments – chances are they are feeling more defensive than they are prepared to tell you. Whereas if they lean forward, picking up their pen and paper to write down notes, they clearly relish the idea of using feedback to help them improve their performance. Your role as their coach is to hold a mirror up for them and reflect back to them what you notice so they can understand how *they* are truly feeling. This process will help the coachee order their thoughts by drawing out themes that encourage them to move a step closer to their goal.

4. BUILDING TRUST AND CONFIDENCE

Now that you understand how to minimize interference, handle different personality types and listen beyond the words, you can begin the all-important business of building a strong coaching relationship. You will need to use all of your social skills to help you build rapport, create a balanced partnership and demonstrate empathy. These are the key steps to building a successful coaching relationship that enables the other person to improve their performance and reach their full potential.

STEP ONE: BUILDING RAPPORT

Establishing rapport is the first step in building a relationship. Building rapport helps you lay the foundation for your future coaching relationship. Without it, your coaching sessions will soon grind to a halt or you will struggle to get off the starting blocks in the coaching process. Good rapport is particularly important if you are coaching someone you do not know very well. As Tony Robbins said, "Rapport is the ability to enter someone else's world, to make them feel that you understand them, that you have a strong common bond." The great news is that there are practical steps you can take to build rapport effortlessly.

HOW TO BUILD RAPPORT

- **Talk their language** – tune in to the phrases they use and try to incorporate them into the conversation when appropriate.
- **Make sure you are on their wavelength** – ask pertinent questions to understand what really makes them tick and help find common ground.
- **Demonstrate genuine interest** – don't just pretend to be interested! You need to really care about their personal development.
- **Summarize what they say** to ensure your understanding of their needs and to demonstrate they have your full attention.
- **Match and mirror their body language** to create trust and respect. This could be nodding when they do or using the same gestures to support a point.
- **Fluctuate your pace and tone** to keep the other person engaged in what you have to say.

Although rapport can be quickly established it can also be easily broken, so avoid the following behaviours:

HOW TO BREAK RAPPORT

- Pretending to listen rather than actively listening.
- Looking like you are in a hurry. With actions like constantly checking your watch or rushing them to make decisions, they will sense that you would rather be elsewhere.
- Making assumptions rather than uncovering the reality of the situation.
- Adding your opinion inappropriately instead of encouraging them to take ownership of the process.
- Being judgemental rather than impartial and using leading questions or asking "why?"
- Getting too personal too soon. Don't be overfamiliar as this could make the other person feel uncomfortable and less likely to open up to you.

STEP TWO:
CREATING A BALANCED RELATIONSHIP

Once you have established rapport, you need to set the relationship up for success by keeping it on an equal footing. This can be particularly challenging for a manager used to being directive when managing their team. So, make sure you have your coaching hat firmly on and remember that you both need to have mutual respect in order to work effectively together.

The diagram below illustrates the importance of equality and mutuality in coaching.

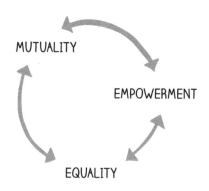

MUTUALITY

EMPOWERMENT

EQUALITY

By seeing each other as equals, you are balancing the conversation and showing the other person you believe in them. Your aim is to be straightforward so you can both be honest and open. This will help establish your credibility and encourage the other person to buy in to the coaching process.

The second element of a balanced relationship is mutuality. Both parties need to benefit from the coaching conversation; you will feel rewarded by their progress and they will recognize that you appreciate their particular objectives and challenges and trust them to find the answers. This empowers the coachee to take responsibility for their actions going forward. You are, in essence, trusting the other person to be the very best that they can be.

STEP THREE:
DEMONSTRATING EMPATHY

The final step in building a relationship is harnessing your empathy so you can put yourself in the other person's shoes. All too often, people confuse empathy with sympathy. However, your role is not to 'be nice' or 'agree' with everything they say. Being empathetic is about seeing things from the other person's perspective to help develop your relationship on a deeper level. This entails listening to their point of view using all your senses so that you can share their experience. It's therefore not surprising that empathy is often described as the 'emotional glue' that holds relationships together – without it, your coaching sessions are likely to come unstuck.

My final piece of advice is about the importance of managing yourself beyond the conversation and honouring your relationship. Always demonstrate that you respect your coachee's confidentiality and make sure you never share any information. This can be difficult to do, especially if, for example, their manager or sponsor asks you about their progress. Remember the contract and that if you betray the coahee's confidence, you are paying lip service to the coaching process.

KEY TAKEAWAYS

I hope this section has helped reassure you that you have the skills for effectively managing yourself in coaching conversations. Here's a quick summary:

- Harness your emotional intelligence to be truly present in the moment, handle different personality types, read beyond the words and build trust and confidence.
- Reflect on the six internal dialogues to remind yourself of the level of interference that can occur during the coaching conversation.
- Draw on your self-knowledge to identify what is likely to distract you and take steps to reduce this.
- Refer to the DISC model to identify the other person's personality type and flex your coaching style accordingly.
- Use silence to slow down the pace of the conversation. This will remind and encourage the coachee to do most of the talking and transfer responsibility to them.
- Listen beyond the words – only 7% of what we communicate comes from our spoken words; the rest is communicated by our tone of voice and body language.
- Always read the other person's body language to check whether it complements, contradicts or emphasizes what they are saying.
- Use your social skills to build rapport, create a balanced relationship and demonstrate empathy.
- Build rapport by talking their language, asking pertinent questions, finding common ground, demonstrating genuine interest and mirroring their body language.
- Avoid breaking rapport by sharing your opinions, making assumptions, being judgemental or getting too personal too soon.

- Set your relationship up for success by focusing on equality, mutuality and empowerment.
- Show the other person you believe in them by treating them as an equal.
- Be proud of the coachee's progress and show them that you recognize their particular objectives and challenges.
- Empower the coachee to take responsibility for their actions.
- Be empathetic by seeing things from the coachee's point of view.
- Finally, always honour your relationship by managing yourself beyond the conversation and respecting your coachee's confidence at all times.

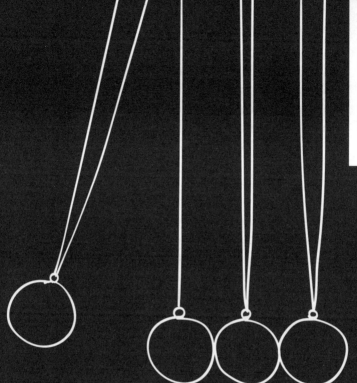

PART FIVE

CREATING
MOMENTUM
FOR CHANGE

In today's 'on-demand' society, people are increasingly looking for instant results or immediate fixes. Unfortunately, changing behaviour doesn't happen overnight – it takes hard work, determination and commitment. Your role as a coach is to create an environment that motivates the other person to achieve and sustain their change in behaviour.

Recognize that there are different strokes for different folks and identify ways to support your coachee as they take on the challenging task of putting their plan into action. As an article by Katzenbach, Steffen and Kronley for the *Harvard Business Review* pointed out, "People will change their behaviour if they see the new behaviour as easy, rewarding and normal." As a coach, it's your responsibility to help the other person break down goals into manageable chunks. Achievements should be celebrated through mechanisms that reward new behaviours that weave changes into daily life so they become a habit.

At the same time, draw on your emotional intelligence – in particular your self-reliance, optimism and self-actualization – to build your sense of purpose. I describe it as the fire in your belly or the reason you get out of bed in the morning. It's the fulfilment that comes from mastering your coaching skills and helping the other person achieve their goals.

This section provides practical advice to help maintain coaching mojo and create momentum for the other person by showing you how to develop optimism, identify motivators, manage the feedback conversation, give meaningful praise and coach your team to achieve a shared goal.

1. DEVELOPING OPTIMISM

It's important to recognize that different things will stand in the way of different people's ability to make progress. These could be self-limiting beliefs such as, "No matter how hard I work, I'll never be good enough," relationships at work, "My boss and I just don't see eye-to-eye" or the individual's mood or temperament at a given time, "I'm feeling stressed and out of control." It's the coach's responsibility to help the other person identify what is standing in the way of their progress. More often than not, these obstacles are negative thought patterns such as over-generalizing, catastrophizing or selective seeing when people dwell on the downsides of a situation.

Fortunately, there are practical steps that retrain the brain to be more objective. By drawing on your optimism and encouraging the person you are coaching to do the same, you can help them become solution-orientated and resilient. Optimists are known to possess personality traits that help them achieve great success in life. When they are optimistic, they are more likely to embrace the unfamiliar, deal well with stress and bounce back from setbacks. This results in happier and healthier individuals with higher levels of productivity and a greater sense of fulfilment.

WHICH WOLF ARE YOU FEEDING?

A powerful story that illustrates the power of optimism is the Cherokee legend of The Two Wolves. The tale begins with a grandfather telling his grandson, "There is a battle between two wolves that live inside us all. One wolf is evil and embodies anger, jealousy, regret, self-pity and guilt. The other wolf is good and represents peace, hope, benevolence, empathy and generosity." The grandson thinks about it for a while and asks, "Which wolf wins?" The grandfather replies, "The one you feed."

In other words, we all have a range of emotions that do battle within our heads. However, by drawing on our optimism and looking for the positives in situations, we can actively choose to feed the good wolf and silence our negative thoughts so we can achieve our full potential. Let's now look in more detail at how to develop optimism.

FOUR STEPS TO HELP DEVELOP OPTIMISM

1. **Retrain your brain to look for the positives** – keep asking yourself, "What's the good I can see here?"
2. **Be solution-orientated** – reframe situations as opportunities rather than problems and think creatively to discover a solution.
3. **Draw on your resilience** – to bounce back from setbacks, take the learnings and plan what you would do differently next time rather than dwelling on negative emotions.
4. **Manage your state and mood** – prevent negative thoughts spiralling out of control by taking regular breaks, exercising or catching up with a friend. This will stop you catastrophizing a situation and leave you feeling re-energized.

EXERCISE

Fill in the table below to take positive steps to stay optimistic and motivated. You can also use this exercise to help the person you are coaching develop their optimism.

WHAT CAN I DO TO DEVELOP OPTIMISM?	WHAT CAN I DO TO MANAGE MY STATE?
Example: Nominate a buddy to help me spot my opportunities for reframing negative situations – review this with them once a week over coffee	*Example: Take a walk in the fresh air every day at lunchtime for at least ten minutes*
...	...
...	...
...	...
...	...
...	...

2. IDENTIFYING KEY MOTIVATORS

In my experience, people are generally highly engaged in the coaching process during the excitement and novelty of the GOAL stage in the GROW model, but their enthusiasm and commitment can start to wane during the REALITY, OPTIONS and WILL ACTION stages. This is where the hard work really kicks in, so it's important that as a coach you understand exactly what motivates the other person. Different people will be motivated by different things. So, avoid the common mistake of presuming that the other person will be motivated by the same things you are. Below is a list of examples of the most common motivators:

- **Material Rewards**: possessions, wealth and a high standard of living
- **Influence**: being in control of people and resources
- **Meaning**: doing things that are believed to be valuable for their own sake
- **Expertise**: seeking a high level of achievement in a specialized field
- **Creativity**: seeking to innovate and be identified with original input
- **Affiliation**: nourishing and rewarding relationships with others at work

- **Recognition**: being recognized and respected by other people
- **Autonomy**: being independent and making key decisions
- **Security**: seeking a solid and predictable future

A great way to help the coachee identify what truly motivates them is to write down each of these nine motivators on individual cards and then ask them to complete the exercise below. Remember to take yourself out of the equation and remain objective as they do it.

EXERCISE

1. Place all nine of the motivator cards on a table in front of your coachee and ask them to prioritize their top three motivators.
2. Ask them to answer the question:

   "What does that motivator mean to you?"

   An example answer could be "autonomy – because it gives me the flexibility to manage my work-life balance."

MY TOP THREE CAREER MOTIVATORS	WHAT THAT MOTIVATOR MEANS TO ME
...	...
...	...
...	...

This exercise is particularly useful to do in the REALITY stage as it can help the coachee understand why they are feeling stuck. For example, if they are motivated by recognition and praise but are doing a back-office role, they may be feeling underappreciated. Whereas if their top motivator is creativity and their job does not allow them to innovate, they could end up feeling frustrated and constrained by their role. By helping the coachee identify what really motivates them, you can spur them on to change the situation. For example, in the case of someone who is motivated by material rewards and influence, they may need a promotion to the next level to keep them motivated and engaged. Your role is, therefore, to help them discover what barriers may be stopping them from getting their promotion.

This simple but extremely powerful tool is useful for yourself too. It will give you a perspective on why you are a coach and will also inform you of any potential bias on your part.

3. GIVING HONEST FEEDBACK

Feedback is described as 'the breakfast of champions' for a reason. It gives the person you are coaching food for thought by helping them hone their skills, reinforce good behaviours, become aware of unhelpful behaviours and stay motivated and engaged. Just as world-class athletes rely on their coaches to seek new ways to raise their game, it's your responsibility to help your coachee move out of their comfort zone and into their stretch zone – their area of best performance. After all, as Bill Gates said, "We all need people who give us feedback. That's how we improve."

However, in my experience, many people shy away from giving feedback because they don't want to upset the apple cart or they fear the emotional reaction their conversation might provoke. This is particularly the case if you are coaching someone internally and you may be concerned about upsetting the relationship. So be brave and front-footed and remember that your goal is to *help* the other person improve their performance – whether it's by closing down a blind spot, boosting their confidence or developing their skills and capability. As their manager (or senior colleague), as opposed to an external coach, you will have more observation points and greater opportunities to give feedback because you see them perform on a day-to-day basis. Therefore, make sure that you give feedback appropriately and authentically.

It can sometimes be difficult to strike the right balance between praise and constructive feedback. Don't be tempted to sugar-coat your key messages. Be honest and fair and make sure you get any performance issues out on the table. This way, you can give the other person the guidance and support they need going forwards to help them work on their areas for development. However, don't just give feedback when things are going wrong. Take the time to give praise where praise is due. It's a human trait to crave recognition and there is nothing better for motivating the other person than giving them meaningful praise for a job well done. We'll look at exactly how to do this later in the section.

WHEN TO GIVE FEEDBACK

You only need to look at websites such as TripAdvisor or Airbnb to recognize the important role feedback plays in our world today. However, for feedback to be powerful it needs to be specific and timely. Avoid general comments such as, "You are a good presenter," and instead say, "I was very impressed by the way you engaged the audience and communicated your key points at our last conference." Your words will carry much more weight if they are rooted in a time and place as the other person will understand the specific behaviour you want to see more of. A great way to help the other person hone a new skill is to feed-back before and after they put it into practice. This way, you are setting them up for success by helping them get their head in the right place beforehand and encouraging them to review their performance afterward so they can keep raising the bar.

Above all, don't just save feedback for the annual performance appraisal. Whereas most individuals crave instant feedback, many companies are still stuck in the cycle of saving feedback for formal reviews.

WHAT YOU SHOULD GIVE FEEDBACK ON

I'm often asked *what* coaches should give feedback on and the answer is anything that the other person can do something about. This could be feedback on their communication style, working practices or more general behaviour. The most important thing is that the feedback is specific and direct. Whenever possible, avoid giving another person's feedback. For feedback to be really effective it needs to come straight from the horse's mouth. The secret to giving meaningful feedback is to ensure it is performance focused as opposed to people focused. In other words, it's not about whether they are a good or a bad person, it's about helping them drive their performance through clear and direct language.

HOW YOU SHOULD GIVE FEEDBACK

In order for feedback to make a real impact on the other person's performance, it's crucial that you tailor it to the particular needs and style of the individual. The feedback framework below will help you deliver feedback in the most effective and meaningful way:

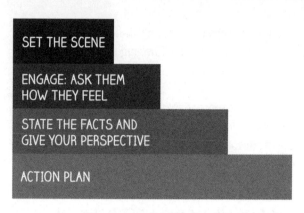

Developmental Feedback Framework

Step One: Set the scene

First, be proactive and introduce the feedback by setting the scene using clear language to describe exactly what feedback you would like to give them. Remember to root it in a set time and place.

> Example scenario: You have been working with your coachee to help them improve their presentation skills and want to give them feedback on how they are progressing. A powerful way to set the scene would be to say, "I'd like to talk to you about how you pitched your idea in the after-lunch slot of our team meeting – in particular, I'd like to focus on how you delivered your key messages, your tone of voice and your body language."

Step Two: Ask them how they feel

A powerful way to engage the other person in the feedback process is to ask them how they feel their performance went. It helps you assess how they view the situation. For example, if they are unduly critical about their skills, it could suggest they still lack confidence. Alternatively, if they are overly positive, it could indicate they have a blind-spot.

Example scenario: Keep the feedback process conversational by asking, "How did you feel presenting in front of the team?" or "Do you feel your presentation went well?" Make sure you are actively listening to their response. This will help you understand their perspective and guide the type of feedback you need to deliver.

Step Three: State the facts and your perspective

Having listened with empathy, you need to use direct and honest language to provide feedback. Don't sugar-coat the facts; use specific examples to illustrate how you felt they performed and what areas – if any – could be improved. Harness your self-control to remove emotion from your voice, maintain eye contact and breathe deeply so that you can speak with confidence. Don't forget to describe the impact their performance had on you and others. It's important they understand the overall impression they gave.

Example scenario: Your feedback statement could be: "Well done – I thought you used confident language when you delivered your key messages to the team. You have worked hard at eliminating 'weak speak' and your tone of voice was much stronger than at the last meeting. This helped to keep your audience engaged in what you had to say. At times you relied too much on your presentation notes which meant you lost eye contact – this suggests you still lack confidence when presenting in front of your colleagues."

Step Four: Agree on an action plan

The final step in the feedback framework is to transfer ownership to the other person by agreeing on next steps. You need to get their input to agree on what actions or steps they are going to commit themselves to start doing, or to stop doing and or in fact to keep doing in order to improve their performance.

Valuable coaching questions you can ask are: "What have you learned?" and "What will you do differently next time?" Make sure the action plan is achievable but stretching. Agree on the support that is needed and make sure you set a clear time frame.

So, in summary, the action plan step is very similar to the 'Option' and 'Will Action' steps of the GROW model.

> Example scenario: Together you both agree that they need to continue to eliminate weak speak and focus on how to improve their body language, maintain eye contact and convey greater confidence when they present. You have agreed to help them rehearse their next presentation ahead of next month's team meeting to help them fine-tune their performance.

The more you practise using this feedback framework, the more confident and comfortable you will feel about giving feedback. While the developmental framework above is applicable to most coaching scenarios, sometimes it is more appropriate to use a more direct approach to giving feedback as shown on the next page.

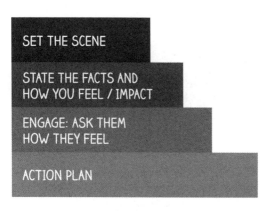

Direct Feedback Framework

Unlike the Developmental Feedback Framework where you set the scene and ask the other person how they feel, with the direct feedback framework, you set the scene and move straight to giving feedback. This is particularly applicable if you already know where your coachee's blind-spots are. For example, in the case of honing presentation skills, if you recognize that the person assumes they have done a great job, whereas you think they have failed to capture their audience's attention, it is more effective to pre-empt them and deliver the difficult message *before* you ask them how they feel. This can be followed by asking coaching questions such as, "How do you feel about the feedback?" so that you can agree on the next steps together.

Confident coaches recognize the need to tailor both feedback frameworks according to the personality type of the person being coached. The DISC table below is an invaluable tool to help you deliver feedback in the most effective way for the four different personality types.

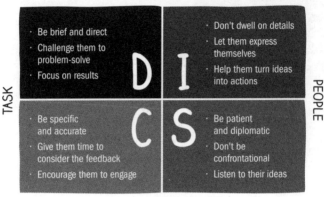

OUTGOING

TASK

PEOPLE

D
- Be brief and direct
- Challenge them to problem-solve
- Focus on results

I
- Don't dwell on details
- Let them express themselves
- Help them turn ideas into actions

C
- Be specific and accurate
- Give them time to consider the feedback
- Encourage them to engage

S
- Be patient and diplomatic
- Don't be confrontational
- Listen to their ideas

RESERVED

The table above shows that D type personalities respond to brief and direct feedback that focuses on results. I types won't want to dwell on the detail and will need help turning their ideas into actions. S types will need you to be patient and diplomatic and will want you to listen to their ideas. And C types will appreciate feedback that is specific and accurate; however, you will need to encourage them to engage with it.

It's important to bear in mind that regardless of personality types, most people react to feedback. This is because humans generally don't like change. The SARAH Curve on the next page demonstrates the stages that most people go through when making the change required as a result of coaching or feedback.

LEVEL OF EMOTION

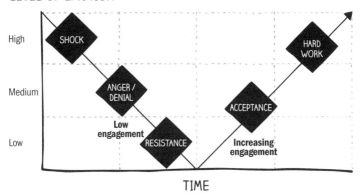

The SARAH Change Curve

As the SARAH Curve illustrates, people may initially experience shock (S) as they come to terms with their situation or feedback. They could then react with anger (A) or denial, preferring to turn a blind eye and ignore the reality of the situation. Next, resistance (R) may creep in – after all, changing behaviour is hard work – and it is not surprising that people are tempted to drag their heels. Once they reach acceptance (A), this is the turning point – they recognize that the feedback will help them up their game and remove barriers that are getting in the way of their progress. The final step is hard work (H) as they commit to putting in the hours to address the feedback and change their behaviour going forwards.

The process of coaching and the role of the coach or person providing the constructive feedback accelerates the amount of time it takes for people to go through the SARAH Curve. It enables them to progress quickly from shock to acceptance so that they can move on smoothly to making a plan to improve their performance.

Exactly how people respond to feedback will depend to a large degree on their personality type. Here are tips on how to handle different people's reactions to challenging feedback:

- D Types are most likely to respond to feedback by asking questions. As their coach, don't be defensive; listen to what they have to say and respond appropriately.
- I types are more likely to overreact to feedback; therefore, try to remove any emotion from the conversation and give them time to air their views.
- S types generally like to reflect on feedback and will need you to be patient. Remember to ask questions to help them process what you have said.
- C types may initially be silent, so at the appropriate time ask questions to understand their perspective and give them time to consider their action plan.

Despite your best efforts, if you find the coachee is not following up on their actions, see it as an opportunity to give them further feedback. Re-engage with them by asking questions to help understand what is stopping them from moving forwards. Try to break the action plan down into manageable chunks and work together to agree on a new timescale and follow-up process.

GIVING MEANINGFUL PRAISE

As mentioned earlier, we all want to be recognized and rewarded by our managers and colleagues. In fact, according to a report from the Boston Consulting Group, appreciation of our work is the number one factor for employee happiness. It's therefore not surprising that giving your coachee meaningful praise is a powerful technique to help motivate and encourage them to reach their full potential.

Remember, people are different, so use your knowledge of the other person's personality type to give them meaningful praise. I've put together the guidelines below to help you:

D Types are fuelled for results and driven by their ego. Keep this front-of-mind when you give them meaningful praise. Focus the praise on their individual contribution and tell them how they have impacted the results. This will continue to stimulate their desire to improve and deliver even better results.

I Types are motivated by what people think of them. So whenever possible, give them public recognition for work well done; this will inspire them to keep improving their performance. Creating or giving them the forum to share their successes can work wonders for their momentum.

S Types will value praise if it is sincere, otherwise they may struggle to believe it. Create a safe environment to deliver the praise – as you don't risk embarrassing them in front of others. Don't be surprised if they downplay their contribution by saying, "It wasn't just me – it was the team."

C Types are considered and conscientious, so praise them for their accuracy, perseverance and hard work. As more introverted individuals, try to praise them in private – if, however, you need to do it publicly, give them warning so they are prepared for it.

By harnessing your adaptability and optimism to give the coachee praise in a way that is meaningful for them, you are setting them up for success by motivating them to move closer to achieving their goals.

4. COACHING YOUR TEAM

I want to finish this section by looking at how momentum can be created to make a change for your team as a whole. There are plenty of coaching models that can help you, but I find the most effective one is the Forming, Storming, Norming and Performing model which was first published by psychologist Brian Tuckman in the *Psychological Bulletin* in 1965.

In this model there are four stages in a team's journey:

Forming: when a team first meets and learns about potential opportunities and challenges. People are generally on their best behaviour and focused on themselves as opposed to the team as a whole.

Storming: when people in the team grow in confidence and begin to voice their opinions – as a result, through conflict or personality clashes, the team will discover what it is like to work together.

Norming: when people begin to resolve their differences, toler-ate other team members' ways of working and appreciate their strengths and what everyone can bring to the table. At this point, the team will begin to work towards a common goal.

Performing: when everyone in the team understands what is expected of them and works together as a unit to achieve shared goals and objectives.

As a manager, you need to use your emotional intelligence to judge exactly where your team is on this journey. Remember, this can vary depending on the particular challenge they are facing or whether someone new has joined the team. Your role is to constantly evaluate their performance so that you can support them along the way – both individually and collectively.

You can draw on everything you have learned so far in this book and apply it to your team. Use the GROW model to set a common goal, establish the reality of the situation your team is facing, explore new opportunities and ways of working and put a plan of action together that allows the team to perform to the best of their ability. Be mindful of the different personality types on your team and flex your communication style accordingly. It can be challenging to be in the team and simultaneously coach members, so I often recommend using a facilitator to help with team coaching. Finally, encourage everyone in your team to give and receive meaningful feedback so they are motivated and inspired to keep raising their game.

KEY TAKEAWAYS

The ability to build and maintain momentum is a crucial skill for any coach. Here's a quick refresher on the key points covered to achieve this:

- Draw on your emotional intelligence to build momentum for yourself as a coach and the person you are coaching.
- Help the other person change their behaviour by coaching them so that their actions are easy, rewarding and normal.
- Develop your optimism by retraining your brain to 'feed the good wolf' and look for the positives in a situation.
- Be resilient and bounce back from setbacks by taking the learnings and moving forwards.
- Manage your mood by taking regular breaks, doing exercise or socializing with friends to help banish any negative thoughts.
- Identify your coachee's key motivators using the motivator card exercise.
- Stay objective; don't just presume the coachee will be motivated by the same things you are.
- Use your knowledge of the coachee's personality type to keep motivating them as they put their plan into action.
- Give your coachee honest feedback to help them hone their skills, reinforce good behaviours and raise awareness of unhelpful behaviours so that they stay motivated and engaged.
- Make sure your feedback is rooted in time and place and is given regularly – don't just save it for their annual appraisal.
- Remember that you can give your coachee feedback on *anything* that they can do something about.
- Tailor the feedback to the needs of the individual using the developmental feedback framework for a guide.

- Adopt the direct feedback framework when you recognize the other person has a blind-spot that you need to make them aware of.
- Use the SARAH Curve to understand how people respond to feedback so that you can support them as they adapt to change.
- Refer to the DISC framework to identify how to handle different personality types' reactions to challenging feedback.
- Use the Forming, Storming, Norming and Performing model to understand where your team is on their journey and create momentum to work together towards a common goal.
- Encourage everyone on your team to give and receive feedback so you can keep raising the bar.

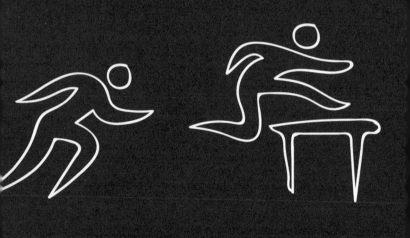

PART SIX

KEEPING
COACHING FIT

Congratulations on reaching the final section of *The Coaching Book* – you should now have a clear understanding of the powerful role coaching can play in *helping people discover a new way forwards to fulfil their potential and maximize their performance.*

I hope I have succeeded in making coaching theory accessible by providing easy-to-use tools and techniques that you can weave into everyday life to set yourself up for coaching success. You should be well positioned to develop a coaching mindset, build rapport and trust, adopt a disciplined approach, manage yourself during the coaching conversation and create momentum for change.

However, be under no illusion, remembering to do all of this when coaching can be challenging. You will need to keep fit for coaching by applying these principles on a day-to-day basis with colleagues and friends until they become second nature. Only then will you feel truly confident and authentic as a coach.

In this section, I will focus on how to fine-tune coaching performance by identifying the type of coach you want to be, managing unconscious bias so you remain objective, adopting a plan, do, review and asking for feedback to keep improving your coaching performance.

1. DISCOVERING THE TYPE OF COACH YOU WANT TO BE

The more coaching hours you put in, the more comfortable you will feel wearing your coaching hat. Referring back to the learning journey in Part 2, your aim is to progress from conscious competence, when developing your newly acquired coaching skills, to unconscious competence, when your skills are firmly embedded and have become a habit. Only at this point will you have the bandwidth to discover the type of coach you want to be. You may decide that you get the greatest sense of fulfilment as a commercial skills coach or discover that confidence or performance coaching plays more to your strengths. In either case, you need to draw on your self-awareness so you can be true to yourself and coach in an authentic manner. This is easier said than done, as psychologist Brené Brown explains in her book, *The Gifts of Imperfection*, "Authenticity is the daily practice of letting go of who we're supposed to be and embracing who we are."[5]

The more confident you feel as a coach, the happier you will be to reveal the true you. If, for example, you are an extrovert, chances are you are more likely to be a coach who enjoys challenging the other person, whereas if you are more introverted your natural inclination is probably to adopt a more supportive approach. It's important to bear in mind that neither approach is better or worse than the other – it really is a matter of preference. Challenging coaches will be happy to ask the tough questions and are more likely to be fast-paced, whereas supportive coaches tend to be more reflective and give the other person greater time to think.

As a coach, you can obviously adapt your style according to the person you are coaching – however, the more experienced you become, the more likely you are to feel authentic by coaching in a particular manner. In which case, if you feel your coaching style isn't the right fit for the other person or there is a lack of chemistry, you need to have the confidence to call it and recommend they are coached by someone else instead.

2. MANAGING UNCONSCIOUS BIAS

Whether we like it or not, we all have prejudices that can skew our judgement and ability to be objective and impartial. Our unconscious brain is hardwired to instinctively categorize people or things together to help us make sense of the world. Biases can be based on gender, age, skin colour, social status, nationality, job title and so on. They are those deeply engrained thoughts in our unconscious mind that explain why we might be automatically drawn to people who are more like ourselves or respond more negatively to a group of people less like ourselves. As part of your journey to becoming a confident and authentic coach, you need to use self-awareness and self-control to manage unconscious bias.

The first step to overcoming unconscious bias is to use your self-awareness to identify any prejudices. Perhaps, for example, your unconscious bias is that you are wary of D type personalities based on your previous experience of a boss who was direct and dominant. The next step is to leverage your self-control and respond rather than react to any biases. This means fine-tuning your performance so that you stay objective instead of making a snap judgement. The more types of people you coach, the more likely you are to refrain from judgement and be open-minded. One of the delights of coaching is appreciating how complex and unique people actually are.

3. ADOPTING THE PRINCIPLE OF PLAN, DO, REVIEW

A powerful way to help take your coaching from good to great is to adopt the principle of plan, do and review. Just as it is your responsibility to encourage the person you are coaching to keep raising the bar, so it is coaching best practice to keep challenging yourself to up your game.

In my experience, coaches are usually good at planning for a coaching session but often fail to take the time to review what went well and what could be improved for next time. For example, did you notice that you were making a snap judgement rather than staying impartial, or did you find yourself offering advice instead of helping the other person come up with their own ideas?

PLAN

DO

REVIEW

I have put together a Coaching Diary template below to help you prepare ahead for your next coaching session, evaluate your performance during the coaching conversation itself and focus on the areas for improvement going forwards.

PREPARATION	PERFORMANCE			FOCUS
To Be Present And Confident	Session Impression	Comments	Score	Improvement Areas
...	**C**ontracting	...	...	...
	Open Relationship			
...	**A**sking Questions	...	...	...
...	**C**oncentrating/ Listening	...	...	...
...	**H**onest Feedback	...	...	...

The Coaching Diary Template

Be brave and disciplined – make sure you fill in the diary each time you have a coaching session.

1. Use the preparation box to write down ways to help you focus so you are truly present in the moment.
2. Reflect on your performance afterwards and score yourself accordingly, writing down any relevant comments.
3. Finish by thinking of ideas that you can deploy to improve your coaching performance. A great way to do this is to adopt the GROW model for yourself.

Another tool to help you improve your coaching skills is the coaching log shown below. You can use this live in the moment to help record what is being said in the meeting. Just make sure you confirm with the other person beforehand and make sure they are happy for you to make notes as they talk. This will help prepare going forwards as you will be able to keep track of the progress that has been made. This is particularly helpful if you are coaching lots of different people.

GOAL	REALITY	OPTIONS	WILL ACTION
...	...	...	...
...	...	...	...
...	...	...	...
...	...	...	...

The Coaching Log

4. GETTING FEEDBACK

The previous section focused on the importance of giving feed-back and meaningful praise to motivate people and improve their performance. As a coach, you will need to practise what you preach – so demonstrate how much you value feedback by asking for it in return. Remember, feedback will help you identify any blind spots or areas for development. It can also boost confidence and reassure you that you are on the right track.

Follow the five steps below to help you ask for feedback:

- **Consider the timing** – use your judgement to decide whether to ask for feedback formally using a form at the end of a series of sessions or informally at the end of each session by asking the coachee how they felt it went.
- **Be specific in what you ask** – it can be difficult for a coachee to give feedback on your performance so make it easier for them by breaking it down into detailed questions such as, "Describe how you feel these coaching sessions have helped you," or, "What would make your coaching sessions even more effective?"

- **Identify the best way to gather the feedback** – this will vary according to the personality type of the person you are coaching. D types are likely to be direct and want to lead the conversation, I types might prefer to chat informally over a coffee, whereas C and S types are more likely to prefer to fill in a form.
- **Be grateful** – remember, feedback is a gift and will help you improve. So, don't be defensive or argue with what your coachee has to say or they won't feel comfortable giving feedback going forwards.
- **Really listen** – draw on your emotional intelligence to actively listen to what the other person has to say. A great way to ensure you are truly present is to make notes as they talk. This will help you digest the feedback and be a useful record later as you make a plan of action.

It's important to bear in mind that you will almost certainly experience a response to the feedback, so remember to draw on your self-control as you listen to the other person. The techniques below will help you manage your reaction:

- **Digest before responding:** take a moment to really absorb what is being said rather than responding with a knee-jerk reaction.
- **Put yourself in other person's shoes**: remind yourself that it takes courage to give feedback, so be appreciative of what they have to say.
- **Step outside of yourself**: depersonalize the feedback process by adopting an objective mindset.
- **Ask questions to gain clarity**: don't dismiss the other person's feedback out of hand – use questions to understand the situation more clearly and identify ways you can improve.

- **Keep your strengths and talents top of mind**: this will ensure you keep a sense of balance and perspective.
- **Remember the positive intent behind the feedback**: the role of feedback is to help you reach your full potential so don't dwell on the negatives or view it as personal criticism.

In addition to getting regular feedback, another powerful way to keep fit for coaching is to be coached yourself. This is particularly useful if you are an internal coach as it enables you to bounce ideas off someone more experienced and remind you what it feels like to be a coachee. As a qualified trainer and coach with more than 15 years' coaching experience, I still get enormous benefit from being coached on a regular basis. It ensures I keep my skills up to date, so I stay at the very top of my game.

It's important to remember that you are a work in progress. So, keep this book close to hand and use it to support your journey to becoming a confident coach. This way, you can refer back to the practical advice in these pages.

I hope that I have succeeded in sharing with you the immense sense of fulfilment that comes from helping other people become the best that they can be. As a manager, there can be no greater privilege than helping the people in your team reach their full potential. As American basketball coach John Wooden said, "A good coach can change a game, a great coach can change a life."

KEY TAKEAWAYS

Here's a final reminder of the steps you can take on a day-to-day basis to help you keep fit for coaching:

- Put coaching theory into practice by weaving it into your daily life whether it's with your team, colleagues or friends.
- Draw on your confidence and self-awareness to identify your authentic coaching style.
- Put in the coaching hours to help discover whether you want to be a more supportive or a more challenging coach.
- Harness your self-awareness to identify any unconscious bias, then leverage your self-control to respond rather than react to these prejudices and remain objective.
- Adopt the principle of plan, do, review to keep raising your coaching game.
- Use the Coaching Diary template to prepare for your next coaching session, evaluate your performance during the coaching conversation itself and brainstorm ways to improve going forwards.
- Keep track of different coaching sessions using the Coaching Log – this will help you prepare effectively for each coaching session.
- Practice what you preach and ask for feedback from your coachees to help identify any blind-spots or areas for development.
- Identify the best way to gather feedback, consider the timing and be specific about what you want feedback on.
- Draw on your emotional intelligence to listen with empathy to the feedback and absorb what the other person has to say.
- Try not to be defensive or take feedback as personal criticism – view it as a gift that enables you to grow and develop as a coach.
- Consider being coached yourself to keep honing your skills so that you can reach your full potential.

FURTHER READING

- *A Theory of Human Motivation*, Abraham Maslow, 1943
- *Drive: The Surprising Truth About What Motivates Us*, Daniel Pink, 2011
- *Eat That Frog – 21 Great Ways To Stop Procrastinating And Get More Done In Less Time*, Brian Tracy, 2007
- *Effective Modern Coaching*, Myles Downey, 2015
- *Emotional Capitalists: The Ultimate Guide For Developing Emotional Intelligence For Leaders*, Dr Martyn Newman, 2014
- *Emotional Intelligence Coaching*, Stephen Neale, Lisa Spencer-Arnell & Liz Wilson, 2015
- *Emotional Intelligence: Why It Can Matter More Than IQ*, Daniel Goleman, 1996
- *50 Top Tools for Coaching*, Gillian Jones and Ro Gorell, 2015
- *How To Win Friends And Influence People*, Dale Carnegie, 1936
- *Lean In – Women, Work and The Will to Lead*, Sheryl Sandberg, 2013
- *Mindset – The New Psychology of Success*, Carol Dweck, 2006
- *7 Habits of Highly Effective People*, Stephen Covey, 2004
- *Start with Why: How Great Leaders Inspire Everyone To Take Action*, Simon Sinek, 2011
- *Silent Messages: Implicit Communication of Emotions and Attitude*, Albert Mehrabian, 1971
- *The Challenger Sale*, Matthew Dixon & Brent Adamson, 2011
- *The Chimp Paradox*, Steve Peters, 2012
- *The Coaching Habit*, Michael Bungay Stanier, 2016
- *The Effective Executive*, Peter Drucker, 2007
- *The Gifts of Imperfection*, Brené Brown, 2010

- *The Inner Game of Tennis*, Tim Gallwey, 2015
- *The Inner Game of Work*, Tim Gallwey, 2000
- *The Little Book of Big Coaching Models*, Bob Bates, 2015
- *The Little Book of Coaching*, Ken Blanchard and Don Shula, 2002
- *The Mindfulness Book: Practical Ways To Lead A More Mindful Life*, Dr Martyn Newman, 2016
- *The Influence Book: Practical Steps to Becoming a Strong Influencer*, Nicole Soames, 2018
- *The Negotiation Book: Practical Steps to Becoming a Master Negotiator*, Nicole Soames, 2017
- *The Tao of Coach*, Max Landsberg, 1996
- *Thrive*, Arianna Huffington, 2016
- *Time To Think – Listening To Ignite The Human Mind*, Nancy Kline, 2002
- *Who Moved My Cheese?* Spencer Johnson, 1999
- *Why Should Anyone Be Led by You?*, Robert Goffee & Gareth Jones, 2015
- *Women Don't Ask*, Linda Babcock & Sara Laschever, 2007
- *Working With Emotional Intelligence*, Daniel Goleman, 1998

REFERENCES

[1] Carnegie Institute of Technology carried out research that showed that 85% of our financial success was due to human engineering personality and the ability to communicate, negotiate and lead – only 15% was due to technical capability

[2] *The Inner Game of Work*, Tim Gallwey, 2000

[3] *The Challenger Sale*, Matthew Dixon & Brent Adamson, p 141, 2011

[4] *Silent Messages: Implicit Communication of Emotions and Attitudes*, Albert Mehrabian, 1981

[5] *The Gifts of Imperfection*, Brené Brown, 2010

ACKNOWLEDGMENTS

It wouldn't be possible to write a book about coaching without thanking the hundreds of people I've coached during my career. Each and every coaching relationship has opened up my eyes to the powerful role coaching plays in changing people's behaviours and making a lasting difference to their lives. As someone who is passionate about setting people up for success, I feel very privileged to have worked with these inspiring individuals as they discovered their own way forwards. There really can be no greater sense of fulfilment than helping someone reach their full potential.

Thank you to my fantastic team at Diadem Performance for their continued enthusiasm and commitment. I feel incredibly lucky to work with a group of people who possess the same coaching mindset and desire to help people be the very best that they can be. By working together to share coaching best practice, we are able to practise what we preach and keep raising our coaching 'bar'.

Thanks again to my wonderful family – my husband James, daughters Talya and Amelie and my parents. I really couldn't do all that I do without your unfailing love and support. Finally, thanks to Martin Liu, Niki Mullen, Sara Taheri and Susan Furber at LID Publishing for ensuring that writing my third book was as enjoyable and seamless a process as writing my first.

ABOUT THE AUTHOR

NICOLE SOAMES is a highly qualified coach and emotional intelligence practitioner. She gained extensive commercial experience during 12 years of managing large sales teams at Unilever and United Biscuits, followed by 15 years developing and delivering training programmes around the world. In 2009, Nicole founded Diadem Performance, a leading commercial skills training and coaching company. With over 100 clients across the globe, Diadem has helped many thousands of people become *commercial athletes* in influencing and selling, negotiation, account management, marketing, presenting, strategy, coaching, leadership and management.

Nicole's charismatic and energetic coaching style and ability to drive change enables people from a diverse range of organizations to think and act outside their comfort zone and unlock their true potential. Nicole is also the best-selling author of *The Negotiation Book* and *The Influence Book*, both part of the Concise Advice Series from LID Publishing. For more information about Nicole's books, visit **www.nicolesoamesbooks.com.**

Get in touch regarding you or your team.

Follow Nicole on Twitter **@diademperform**
Or visit the website **www.diademperformance.com**

FROM THE
SAME AUTHOR

The Negotiation Book
LID Publishing, 2017

The Influence Book
LID Publishing, 2018